CHINA

ET

Lhasa ○ ● Drigung

Arunachal
Pradesh

Namdapha
●

Patkai
hills

Gurudong-
mar lake ●

Taktshang
monastery

DZONG
VALLEY

Sikkim

Tawang ○

Gangtok ○ ● Tsomgo
lake

● Thimpu

du

BHUTAN

MYANMAR

BANGLADESH

UNKNOWN
HIMALAYAS

Published in India by
Roli Books in arrangement with
Roli & Janssen BV, The Netherlands
M-75, Greater Kailash-II Market,
New Delhi 110 048, India.
Phone: ++91-11-29212271, 29212782 , 29210886
Fax: ++91-11-29217185
Email: roli@vsnl.com; Website: rolibooks.com

ISBN: 978-81-7436-566-8

Editors: Amit Agarwal & Dipali Singh
Design: Supriya Saran
Production: Naresh Nigam & Kumar Raman

Printed and bound in Singapore

Preceding page: A monk's shoes at Diksit monastery
in Ladakh.

Facing page: The rolling grasslands of eastern Tibet stretch
behind a horseman on a white stallion.

UNKNOWN HIMALAYAS

HIMANSHU JOSHI

Lustre Press
Roli Books

CONTENTS

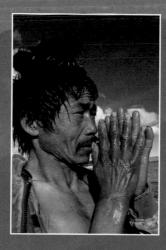

The Himalayas, the youngest mountain chain in the world, have always exerted an irresistible pull on the imagination of travellers. With innumerable valleys and many rivers hiding among the world's highest peaks, the 2500-kilometre length of the Himalayas is a treasure trove of geological and cultural diversity. Probing the various folds of the mountain range is not only fascinating, but also an enriching cultural experience. The exposure to customs and places that have little link with the outside world is akin to taking a peek into time gone by.

This book is a celebration of these nooks and corners of the Himalayas that still continue to preserve and conserve their culture and natural surroundings. It is not that these places — mostly hidden from prying eyes — have not changed over time. They have, but the change is very gradual. This may be due to the remote location of a place or the closed traditions of its inhabitants, or just plain ignorance on our part. These places and people are a window to life that respects nature and strives to live in harmony with it — not in conflict with it as many of us do.

Left: The Lingshed trekking trail in Ladakh. Lingshed is one of the remotest villages in Ladakh.

Top: The work-worn face and heirloom necklaces of a woman in the hidden valley of Humla in Nepal.

The book is divided into nine chapters, with each chapter devoted to a region in the Himalayas. From the high-altitude Ladakh region of Jammu and Kashmir to Arunachal Pradesh, the eastern tip of the Himalayan range, we travel west to east, observing the natural splendour en route and delving into the traditional, cultural and social practices of the indigenous people.

But how does one reach these places? It is always easier to delve into the unknown if you understand the known. Therefore, we first visit the known, tourist-friendly hub of the region we want to explore. This hub gives an introduction to the region and its people and that, in turn, helps us make sense of its hidden secrets. In each chapter, we start from the main hub – for example, Leh in Ladakh or Kathmandu in Nepal – explore the places worth visiting in and around the hub, before taking the road less travelled. The journey could be to a place less visited or a peep into a culture that is less known.

We start with the Ladakh region of Jammu and Kashmir where, after exploring around Leh, we try to observe the lives of two little known tribes of the region – the Drogpas (who claim to be descendants of pure Aryans) and the Changpas (a nomadic tribe that roams the barren Changthang). For the second journey into the Ladakh region, we go to the remote Zanskar valley, which sees only a small trickle of outside visitors.

The next stop is the beautiful Kashmir valley. We start off with Srinagar and then take a lake circuit of the valley, visiting the famous Dal, the lesser known Wular and the little known Manasbal lakes. What follows is the trek up to the Amarnath shrine – this houses the mythical Shivling (phallus of Lord Shiva worshipped by Hindus) high up in the mountains that is formed and shaped every year by nature.

The third chapter takes us to Himachal Pradesh and its capital Shimla, where we take in the sights and sounds of the

Top: A Buddha statue in Ladakh.

Facing page: The Dhankar fort complex perches on a 3870-metre spur that projects into the main Spiti valley and ends in a precipice.

old summer capital of the British Raj and then slowly wind our way along the famous Hindustan-Tibet road, passing through Rampur Bushair, Kinnaur and finally stepping into the spectacular Spiti – a place that time hasn't changed. A visit to the Ki monastery in Spiti valley with its unique honeycomb structure, alongwith Tabo monastery, called the Ajanta of the Himalayas, brings this rugged yet beautiful region alive.

The next journey is along the holy Ganga (Ganges) river in the state of Uttarakhand. We go up the river from Rishikesh and visit the glacier at Gaumukh, a holy spot for Hindus, from where the Ganga originates as Bhagirathi. We undertake a trek to the mysterious lake of Roopkund, where centuries-old skeletons can still be seen. With high Himalayan peaks like Nanda Devi, Trishul and Nanda Ghunti ringing the lake, it is indeed a journey into the unknown realms of life. From the Garhwal region of the state, we then move into Kumaon to

visit places like Kasauni, Baijnath and Binsar, which combine the natural beauty and cultural diversity of the region.

We cover two other Indian states of Sikkim and Arunachal Pradesh in the North-East. In Sikkim, after a stay in Gangtok, we try to understand the life and traditions of Lepchas, the original inhabitants of the state. We then visit the high-altitude lakes of the state that are at once inviting yet mysterious. In Arunachal Pradesh, we go to Itanagar, and then on to Bomdila in the West Kameng district, which is known as the coldest place in the state. In the second part, we try to make our way into the thick rainforests of Namdapha in search of the elusive tiger. In fact, Namdapha is the only forest in India where one can find nine types of cats, right from the celebrated tiger to the small yet beautiful marbled cat.

Outside India, we visit Nepal, the land of high peaks, Bhutan, the Land of the Thunder Dragon, and Tibet, the

Rooftop of the World. While Nepal attracts a lot of visitors from all over the world, we move away from the Kathmandu valley after a short stay to go to the two least visited areas of Nepal – Humla and Dolpo. In Tibet, we start off in Lhasa with its gleaming Potala Palace, bustling bazaars and age-old temples before going on to the mysterious trails where pilgrims throng to circumambulate the sacred mountains. We also focus on the sky burials of Tibet, where the dead are chopped and fed to the vultures. In Bhutan, we visit the Tiger's Nest or the Taktshang monastery, and then try to learn about dzongs, a distinctive type of fortress architecture found only in Bhutan.

This book is essentially a journey to places that march to a different beat, have their own imaginations and the people inside live in their own, different and enviable world.

Top: A detail from the Labrang gompa in Phodong, north Sikkim.

Bottom: A blue water creek enters the brown waters of Zanskar river in Ladakh.

Facing page: A dancer with a skull mask takes part in a religious festival in Ladakh.

Following pages 12–13: The setting sun lights up a rock face with the carved mantra – '*Om mani padme hum*', the mantra of the bodhisattva of compassion, Avalokiteshvara.

LADAKH
THE MYTHICAL SHANGRI-LA

The highest desert in the world, the breathtakingly beautiful Ladakh is a land of myth and silence, full of centuries-old hidden treasures. While its monasteries inspire awe, some of its tribes and communities, such as the Changpas and Drogpas, and far-flung parts such as Zanskar, are fascinating in that they are still off the beaten track.

Preceding page 14: Old chortens in the foreground lead the way to the 15th-century Thikse monastery, a 12-storey building that is home to a nunnery and ten temples.

Preceding page 15: A door at Diksit monastery with sculpted miniature heads.

Leh. The name brings with it a whiff of the exotic. And so it was for a better part of this century owing to its remote geographical location and tough terrain. Spread along a valley in the Ladakh region of the state of Jammu and Kashmir, Leh was the first major town in the trans-Himalayan region of India that came to the notice of tourists. At an altitude of 3650 metres and surrounded by high mountains, Leh was unlike any other Himalayan destination in India. The raw and stark landscape was awe-inspiring and spellbinding at once, and the colourful attire of the people and their unique way of living indeed raised visions of the mythical Shangri-La.

Leh is located in the Indus valley at a crossroads of the old trading routes from Kashgar, Tibet, and Kashmir. Its importance as a trading town lessened with the partition of British India, and ended with the closure of the border in 1962 during the Sino-Indian war. But today it has become a bustling tourist town, with large numbers of Kashmiri traders. As it is a small town, one can easily get to most places on foot. The old town is a compact area of

Left: Rugged mountains rising steeply above a valley in Ladakh.
Top: The wet main street of Leh, with Leh Palace rising above the town.

mud brick houses and narrow lanes directly to the east of Main Bazar. Changspa is the agricultural 'suburb' northwest of the centre, with many guesthouses.

Though Leh is linked by air, because of its high altitude, surface travel is highly recommended for better acclimatization. There are two road approaches to Leh, one from Manali in Himachal Pradesh in the south, and one from Srinagar in the west. Both routes pass through spectacular scenic vistas and both require two-day journeys.

The main advantage of taking the road from Srinagar is that it runs at a lower altitude, and thereby reduces the risk and severity of altitude sickness. It is also open longer – normally from the beginning of June to October – and follows the traditional trade route between Ladakh and Kashmir, which passes through many picturesque villages and farmlands. The journey takes two long days, with an overnight stop in Kargil.

The route from Manali to Leh is more commonly taken by tourists. It takes two days, normally with an overnight stop either in Keylong (altitude 3500 metres) or in tented accommodation in Sarchu (4200 metres) or Pang (4400 metres). On the route are three of the highest road passes in the world – Baralacha, Tanglangla and Namika La . The scenery is fantastic, though it is definitely not for the faint-hearted. It is accessible from mid-July to end-September, and is blocked by snow the rest of the year.

Leh, the capital of Ladakh, has many monasteries and stupas. But what catches the eye of the visitor first is the Leh Palace, an imposing nine-storey structure on top of a hill commanding a grand view of Leh town. Though in ruins now, the palace still has enough grandeur to speak of its rich past. Built in the 17th century by Singey Namgyal, the ruler of Ladakh, it displays features of the typical Tibetan architectural style and is said to have inspired the famous Potala Palace of Lhasa in Tibet, built half a century later. Crowning the Namgyal Tsemo, another peak overlooking the town, are the ruins of a fort, a royal residence built by King Tashi Namgyal in the 16th century.

Broadly speaking, there are two sects of priests or lamas in Ladakh. One is that of the 'Red Hat' lamas, who practise original Buddhism (they wear red hats at the time of ceremonies). In the 15th century, reforms were introduced in the monasteries and the lamas who belong to the reformed order are known as 'Yellow

Preceding pages 18–19: Stakna monastery, built in the early 17th century, rises above the winding Indus.

Facing page: Sculpture of Maitreya, the future Buddha, at Thikse monastery, near Leh.

Top left: Twists and turns on the road to Lamayuru monastery, 130 kilometres from Leh.

Top right: Built in 1430, Namgyal Tsemo gompa is believed to be the earliest royal residence in Leh. It straddles a hilltop behind the Leh Palace and provides some of the best views of the Leh valley.

Hat' lamas, who observe celibacy, among other things. Irrespective of the sect, the power of faith is evident for all to see. All across the land are monasteries, chortens, prayer wheels and mani (prayer) walls covered with smooth river stones, all carefully carved with prayers and polished to a gloss. Faded and torn prayer flags flutter from the most inaccessible of heights. The prayer wheels contain reams of the prayer *'Om mani padme hum'* written over a million times. In the world of Ladakh, the landscape is surreal, the air is still, and the squeak of a prayer wheel is answered by the single resounding stroke of a gong, from an unseen monastery in the rock face.

Most travellers use Leh as a base to visit the numerous gompas (Buddhist monasteries) of Ladakh. Landing at Leh airport, one is greeted by the spectacular sight of the Spituk gompa on a hill adjacent to the runway. Spituk is a thousand years old; the climb up is steep but the magnificent view from the top makes it worthwhile. From the back of the monastery one can look down on the winding Indus and a sprawling green village topped with willows and poplars. The monastery has a large statue of Lord Buddha and a natural rock formation of the Hindu goddess, Kali.

Barely 6 kilometres from Leh is one of the oldest monasteries in Ladakh – the Shey gompa. Built on a huge rock, it was once attached to the summer palace of the rulers. While the abandoned palace lies in ruins, the monastery is well-preserved and contains a 12-metre golden Buddha. In the year 1974, the last king of Ladakh passed away in this monastery. The monastery faces the Stok Museum that has, among other things, a collection of the royal family's traditional clothing and jewellery. It is a showpiece for the royal *thangka*s or painted scrolls (nearly 400 years old), crown jewels, dresses, coins, *perak*s (traditional Ladakhi head-dress) encrusted with turquoise and lapis lazuli as well as numerous religious objects.

The Hemis gompa, 45 kilometres from Leh, is the largest and richest in Ladakh. It is a huge, stunningly beautiful building, with long yellow strips fluttering from its front parapet. Hemis is richly embellished all through – right from the main gate, beyond which is a row of prayer wheels, to the beautifully painted parapet that surmounts the gompa. The Hemis monastery also has an important library of Tibetan books and a very impressive and valuable collection of *thangka*s. One of the largest *thangka*s is displayed every twelve years during the festival time.

Every gompa celebrates its festivals in the form of dance dramas or 'devil dances' in winter. These dances are known as Chham or mask dances and are an important part of Buddhist culture. Hemis, however, is the only gompa which has its two-day festival in summer and therefore attracts tourists from all over the world. Lamas wearing rich, brightly coloured gowns and grotesque masks of legendary or mythical characters perform the dances, accompanied by a Ladakhi orchestra. The dances are performed in the courtyard, while the two-storey gompa is packed with visitors. These dances originally celebrated the killing of the cruel Tibetan king, Landgarma by a monk and now symbolize the victory of good over evil.

Hemis to Thikse is a pleasant drive of about an hour. A cluster of houses rises tier upon tier, culminating in the chambers of lamas and the gompa on the hilltop. The monastery is a 12-storey building, all painted in white, ochre and dark red, and houses a nunnery and ten temples. The gompa's main hall is dark and gloomy, but contains a breathtakingly opulent statue of the Maitreya Buddha sitting in the lotus position and studded with gold, turquoise and semi-precious stones. Built in 1980, the 15-metre tall statue is said to be the largest in Ladakh. The walls of the monastery are painted with religious figures, murals, Tibetan

Top: Ceremonial trumpets rend the air during the Nga Chham dance, outside the Naro Photang Puspahari temple in Shey, 15 kilometres from Leh.

Facing page (top): Chham dance being performed in the main courtyard of the Matho monastery, built in the early 16th century.

Facing page (middle): A masked dance performance in the Hemis monastery to celebrate the birth anniversary of Guru Padmasambhava, who introduced Buddhism to Tibet.

Facing page (bottom): Statues of Buddha in various poses at the Thikse monastery. Each gesture signifies an abstract principle.

calendars and the Wheel of Life. There is also a prayer room which contains many books, some of which are handwritten or painted.

Alchi, about 70 kilometres from Leh, is one of Ladakh's most richly painted monasteries. It is the only place where the art manifests marked Kashmiri influences as opposed to the Tibetan style. Unlike other gompas, which are perched on hilltops and are imposing structures, Alchi is a modest-looking structure of mud and tin on flat ground. But the art treasures of wall paintings and sculptures, which this gompa contains, are superb.

The Alchi gompa is said to have been built by Rin Chen Zampo, the great Tibetan teacher who was educated in the monasteries of Bengal and Bihar and spent seventeen years in India. But inscriptions point to its having been built by a member of a Tibetan noble family in the 11th century. The wall paintings here, well preserved over the centuries, are remarkable in concept and workmanship. Also, the village Alchi stands out among other villages of Ladakh with its lush greenery.

In the town of Leh, there is a new white Japanese Shanti Stupa, built in 1983, reachable by a stiff climb to the top (or through a jeepable road). There are excellent views of the town from the top. The architecturally striking Leh mosque, in the main bazaar, is also worth visiting. The Sunni Muslim mosque is believed to stand on land granted by King Deldan Namgial in the 1660s as his grandmother was the Muslim queen of Ladakh.

The oldest monastery in Ladakh is at Lamayuru, located 130 kilometres west of Leh on the Leh-Kargil road. Hemmed in by soaring scree-covered mountains, the whitewashed medieval gompa is perched on top of a near-vertical, unusually eroded cliff. It was founded, according to a legend, by a monk called Naropa, who spent his life meditating on top of a small bit of land emerging from a lake. He wanted a monastery here, so the lake was dried up and the monastery was built. The gompa, founded in the 10th or 11th century, was a major landmark on the old Silk Route. Within walking distance, are some extraordinary lunar-like rock formations. Standing at the start of the main trekking route south to Padum in Zanskar, they look remarkably like the cratered surface of the moon and are commonly referred to as a moonscape. These strange shapes are a big tourist attraction.

The Lamayuru monastery belongs to the Kagyupa Order of Buddhism and is believed to have been wrecked and reconstructed several times. The monastery showcases some of the finest frescos, carpets and *thangka*s you will see in the region. There are caves carved out of the mountain wall and some of the rooms are richly furnished with carpets. The prayer ceremonies in the gompa should not be missed. More than 200 monks live here permanently; they sleep on the ground, and have no windows or electricity in the rooms.

The ideal time to visit the monastery is early morning or late evening when the priests are saying their prayers and doing their mystical chanting. The ringing of bells and blowing of long brass horns lends a magical touch to the whole atmosphere, investing it with a spirituality that is so much a part of Ladakh.

Top: The play of light reveals the 1000-year-old dramatically situated Lamayuru monastery in full glory amidst stark mountains.

Facing page (left): An elderly Ladakhi woman in traditional garb at Lamayuru monastery.

Facing page (right): Nature's work over centuries has eroded the landscape near Lamayuru, making it look like the surface of the moon.

THE UNKNOWN LADAKH
CHANGPAS

In 1994, the Indian government opened some new areas of Ladakh for international tourists though with some restrictions. The period for visiting these areas cannot exceed seven days and tourists are permitted to travel on identified circuits only. It is also obligatory for tour operators and other agencies related to the organized tours that they ensure these rules are followed. These areas have some of the most bewitching Himalayan panoramas and are perfect venues for cultural and adventure tourism. The Khaltse sub-division, the home of the tribe of Drogpas, and Nyoma sub-division, where one can find the Changpa herdsmen, are two of these regions.

The Changpas inhabit the area which has two of Ladakh's biggest lakes – Tso Moriri and Tso Kar. On the banks of Tso Moriri, 230 kilometres from Leh on a diversion from the Leh-Manali road, lies Korzok, a village inhabited by nomadic Changpa herdsmen. It is a hard day's drive from Leh to Korzok and the journey takes nearly eight hours. Tso Moriri literally translates into 'Mountain Lake'. The lake is located in the Rupshu valley, southeast of Leh, at an elevation of about 4511 metres. Oriented

A view of the Changthang highlands from Korzok, a Changpa village, with Tso Moriri lake in the background.

roughly in a north-south direction, the lake measures nearly 20 kilometres in length and is about 8 kilometres at its widest. As is the case with most lakes in the region, it is formed by melting snow, which drains into huge landlocked shallow basins. Luxuriant vegetation covers the lake shore and Tso Moriri has been recognized as a Ramsar site – a wetland site of international importance. It is a breeding ground for numerous species of birds, including the bar-headed geese (their only breeding ground in India) and the black-necked cranes.

The pearl-shaped lake lies in meditative repose, its surface rippling gently in the wind. The blue of the lake waters is almost magical, shifting constantly in response to the game of hide-and-seek played by the clouds and the sun. The mountains on the far shore of the lake are of variegated colours, largely browns and mottled green, their stolidity broken by occasional flashes of purple and violet.

The small village of Korzok sits slightly above the shore of Lake Tso Moriri, at an altitude of 4530 metres. It is here that the Changpas pitch their yak hair tents called *rebos* and tend their herds of yak, goats, sheep and horses. The yak hair tent is very durable and lasts more than ten years. This area serves as the summer home for the Changpas because of the availability of pasture and snowmelt streams. The Changpas move from place to place about four times a year and the burden of carrying the heavy *rebos* is given to the yak.

The plains of the Rupshu valley support the totally nomadic Changpas, who depend on the yak for survival – on its milk, its meat for food, dung for fuel, and wool for clothing and shelter. Changpas have traditionally subsisted on a hearty but unvarying diet consisting almost entirely of roasted barley flour, tea, *chhang* (local brew), meat, salt, milk, butter, and cheese.

The women wear their own version of the Ladakhi *perak*, the traditional head-dress that is a sign of status and wealth. It is a wide strip of leather that is covered with cloth studded with rows of rough-cut turquoise stones, jewelled amulets and silver ornaments. The wide earpieces are made of black lambskin.

The Changpas are the only group in India who use the portable back strap loom for weaving. Each family has a loom, or *thak*, which can be easily set up and used in any location. All woven products, including saddle bags, backpacks, yak hair panels for *rebos*, rugs, carpets and wide woollen panels used for clothing are made with the *thak*.

Apart from animal husbandry and weaving, the Changpas make a livelihood in other ways too. These nomads also collect salt from the impure deposits on the northern shore of the Tso Kar in Rupshu and sell it all over Ladakh. Tso Kar, or the Salt Lake, lies 76 kilometres northwest of Tso Moriri and 290 kilometres from Leh. Located at an altitude of 4480 metres, it is also known as 'White Lake' on account of the salt deposits that collect around it. The lake has no outlet and the water of the lake is extremely brackish.

The lake emerges from the greyish blue haze which envelops the mountains in the afternoon. Even before you reach the lakeshore, you are actually driving across what must have been the ancient lake bed. The lake has shrunk considerably over the years, as is evident from the ancient strandlines etched on the mountainsides which girdle the lake. The water level in the lake long ago must have been a good 20 to 30 metres above the present level.

However, the lake is partly fed by a channel from a smaller freshwater lake. The waters of the Tso Kar lake have no uniform colour, but seem to be made up of number of shades of blue interspersed with shades of green. Sedges and grasses cover its shores and it is riddled with burrows of mammals, such as mountain voles and marmots. If the visitor stays still in one place for a while, the rewarding experience will be watching these creatures at play. Also possible is a glimpse of the Tibetan wild ass, which is quite common here, and a profusion of birds such as the Tibetan sandgrouse and snowfinches.

Facing page (top left): Prayer flags and mani (prayer) stones stand guard over a winter encampment of Changpas.

Facing page (top right): Changpa tribesmen gather for a cleansing ritual performed by a local doctor or *amchi*.

Top: Sheep tracks form a pattern in the Changthang highlands.

Above: Tso Moriri lake, at an altitude of 4511 metres, is one of the largest lakes in Ladakh, and is home to many species of migratory birds.

THE UNKNOWN LADAKH
DROGPAS

Top: The distinctive headgear of the Drogpas, considered to be the last race of pure Aryans in the Indus valley.

Left: Drogpa folk dancers perform their fascinating traditional dance.

To the southwest of Leh, the Khaltse sub-division, the home of the Drogpas, is another new region opened for tourists. The route that is open traverses from Khaltse to the village of Dha via the villages of Dumkhar, Skurbuchan, Hanudo and Biama.

Out of five Drogpa villages in India, only two are open for foreign tourists. The greatest attraction in these areas are the villages of Dha and Biama, which are entirely populated by the remaining Drogpas, considered to be the last race of Aryans confined to the Indus valley. These villages have considerable anthropological and ethnographic importance.

Dha is situated to the southwest of Leh at a distance of 163 kilometres. Being at a lower altitude, Dha is warmer than Leh, which makes it possible to grow a variety of fruit like apricot, apples, walnut and grapes. The features of the Drogpas are pure Indo-Aryan and they appear to have preserved their racial purity down the centuries. Their culture and religious practices are closer in spirit to the ancient pre-Buddhist religion known as Bon. They have preserved their ancient traditions and way of life partly through the celebration of harvests and partly through their songs and hymns. Their language is similar to that spoken in Gilgit in Pakistan-occupied Kashmir and Drogpas are believed to have migrated from Gilgit and settled in the region. Harvest festivals are among the main celebrations of Drogpas. All the people of these villages come out during these days in their colourful traditional dress.

At this stage, with tourism being like a new-born baby, the infrastructure is not adequate in this area. However, there is a good road leading right up to the Drogpa villages and tourists can stay overnight in private guesthouses and or at identified camping sites at Khaltse, Dhomkhar, Skurbuchan, Achinathang, Hanu Do, Biama and Dha villages amid fields of crops and a view of the surrounding mountains.

Top and facing page (bottom): On all major occasions, whether during a festive dance or while praying at a gompa, Drogpa women don their traditional wear, comprising a unique head-dress and jewellery.

Facing page (top): Drogpa women straining water from barley to make a local fermented drink.

THE UNKNOWN LADAKH
ZANSKAR

In Ladakh's neighbouring district of Kargil lies Zanskar, one of the most isolated valleys of the Himalayan region. At a distance of 220 kilometres from Leh, the town of Kargil on the Leh-Srinagar highway lies almost at the centre of the journey. Another 240 kilometres away via Pensi La (4400 metres) lies Padum, the headquarters of Zanskar region. The Zanskar valley lies along the Doda river and the Lungnak river, which is formed by the coming together of the Kargyag and Tsarap rivers near Padum. In turn, these two rivers meet to form the Zanskar river, which then unites with the Indus. Like Ladakh, Zanskar too was closed to outsiders till 1974, but the first motorable road to Zanskar was completed only in 1979.

The Zanskar region is surrounded by high peaks with just

Snow-covered Buddhist chortens mark the entrance of Kharsha monastery in Zanskar.

one outlet – along the Zanskar river that flows through a steep and narrow gorge. The only road into Zanskar is blocked for nearly six to eight months of the year by heavy snowfall. This geographical location has been the main reason for Zanskar's isolation from the rest of the country. But this also provides one of the most fascinating treks for a visitor. When the road is closed, the only way for the people of Zanskar to move out is to walk on the Zanskar river when it freezes in winter. This is today known as the Chadar trek, *chadar* meaning a sheet. Now famous among adventure lovers as a winter trek-route, it has served as a trade route for Zanskari people for centuries.

The trek is indeed an out-of-this-world experience. The surface of the river changes every ten to twelve steps – at one point, it is flat and transparent ice, and then just a few metres ahead, it is frozen froth that ripples. There are little caves by the frozen river in which travellers camp at night. The harsh winters thus provide a benefit to people by curbing the frothing, turbulent Zanskar in its tracks and making it possible to walk on.

Apart from this tough trek, Zanskar has plenty to offer. It has a cultural history that is fascinating in itself. The majority of its inhabitants are Tibetan Buddhists, while the rest are Sunni Muslims whose ancestors settled in Padum and its surroundings in the 19th century. Zanskaris are of mixed Tibetan and Indo-European origin, mainly of the Dard and Mon races.

Padum, at an altitude of 3505 metres, is the hub of the region. This small town nestles on the slopes of a hillock. It was the erstwhile capital of Zanskar and the proof lies in the ruins of an old palace and fort nearby. Ancient rock carvings, dating from the 8th century, can also be seen at the river bank. There are several monasteries in and around Padum. The Stagrimo monastery is an hour's uphill walk while Pibiting has a magnificent stupa. Believed to have been founded by Kanishka (the ruler of the Kushan dynasty) in the 2nd century, the monastery at Sani is 6 kilometres from Padum.

Karsha is the largest monastery in Zanskar and it follows the orthodox Gelugpa sect. It is said to be founded by the great translator Rinchen Zangpo. Some of the best specimens of mural art in Zanskar are found at Karsha and represent five different

Facing page: The honeycomb structure of the Karsha monastery, founded in the 11th century.

Top left: Pensi La glacier, at an altitude of 4400 metres, is the source of Doda river that flows through the valley of Zanskar.

Top right: Horses graze in the Zanskar valley bound by mountains.

Buddha manifestations. Its 500-year old frescoes, housed in the Lhabrang, the chamber where teaching is conducted, are well preserved. There are two ways to reach Karsha, by a two-hour walk from Padum across the Doda river, or through a 17-kilometre long diversion from the Kargil-Padum road.

Another monastery worth visiting is Phugtal. It can only be approached on foot and it takes about three days of walking to reach it. One of the two rare cave monasteries of the region, this large cave consists of many temples that form the monastic complex. Here, it seems, time stopped centuries ago. And it is not only here, for in Zanskar a visitor is transported back into an era when life was much closer to nature and where divinity and the people were inextricably linked together.

Facing page (top left): In winter, when the snow blocks all roads and pathways, horses are the common mode of transport in Zanskar.

Facing page (top right): A Zanskari man adds to a collection of ibex and bharal horns that are considered sacred by the native people.

Facing page (bottom): Phugtal monastery on the Padum-Darcha trail clings to a steep cliff.

Above: A frozen waterfall clearly indicates the extreme cold in the Zanskar valley in winter.

KASHMIR

PARADISE ON EARTH

Synonymous with natural beauty, Kashmir is a valley of lakes and gardens fringed by the Pir Panjal Himalayan chain. While its capital, Srinagar, looks pretty as a picture postcard, Kashmir also offers a mesmerizing and arduous trek up steep mountains to the isolated and holy cave of Amarnath.

Preceding page 40: *Shikara*s (skiffs) are used not only for pleasure rides on the Dal lake in Srinagar, but also for transport of goods such as these flowers.

Preceding page 41: The leaves of the chinar tree turn a blazing orange during autumn.

Preceding pages 42–43: A panoramic view of snow-covered mountains fringing the Wular lake, one of the largest freshwater lakes in Asia.

'**A**gar firdaus bar roo-e zameen ast, Hameen ast-o hameen ast-o hameen ast' ('If there is paradise on earth, it's here, it's here, it's here'). The beauty of Srinagar was encapsulated in these few words by the Mughal emperor, Jehangir, who borrowed his lines from the noted Sufi mystic and poet Amir Khusro. No one could blame him for his outpouring. After the dusty plains of north India, Kashmir surely must have felt like paradise.

Srinagar has this effect and more on everyone who visits the summer capital of Jammu and Kashmir. Every visitor to this valley carries back images that are unforgettable and which he can claim to be his – chinar trees in autumn, the *shikara*s on the lake, beautifully laid-out gardens and the glistening mountains…

The city sprawls across a broad valley ringed by mountains, with three lakes, the Dal, Sona, and the Nagin. The river Jhelum meanders through the city on its way to the wide plains below the valley. The name Srinagar is composed of the words 'Sri' – meaning abundance and wealth – and 'nagar', which means a city.

Srinagar's history dates back to the 3rd century BC, when it formed part of the Maurya empire. Author Kalhan, in his history

Left: The Hazratbal shrine in Srinagar sprawls on the west bank of the Dal lake. The only domed mosque in the city, it houses the hair of Prophet Mohammed.

Above: The scenic splendour of the Pir Panjal ranges on the way to the holy Sheshnag lake in Kashmir.

of Kashmir, *Rajatarangini*, or 'River of Kings', mentions that the old city of Srinagar – now known as Pandrethan – was founded by King Ashoka, the ruler who also introduced Buddhism to the Kashmir valley.

The Hindu and the Buddhist rule of Srinagar lasted until the 14th century, when the entire Kashmir valley, including the city of Srinagar, came under the control of Muslim rulers, including the Mughals. The Mughals ruled over the valley from 1587 to 1752, but the disintegration of the Mughal empire had set in after the death of Aurangzeb in 1707. The valley then came under the rule of the Afghan king, Ahmad Shah Abdali. The Afghans ruled here for sixty-seven years, but when they were defeated by Ranjit Singh, the region passed into the hands of the Sikhs. The two Anglo-Sikh wars and the treaties of Lahore and Amritsar gave the British control over the region. The British then installed Gulab Singh as an independent and sovereign ruler, and Srinagar became part of his kingdom. For a long time, it was one of the several princely states of undivided India, till its accession to India in 1948.

Despite its turbulent history, life in Srinagar has evolved and revolved around its lakes and the river. Though the city was laid towards the northeastern bank of the Jhelum river, it soon expanded to the opposite bank, with the two connected by a number of cantilevered bridges. The first of these, Zaina Kadal, was built by the Shah-Miri King Zain-ul-Abdin. The nine old bridges of the city go by their numbers, each covering a *kadal* or city ward.

The Dal lake, with its fabled blue waters, forms the nerve centre of the city and most of the activity is centred around this natural lake. Described by Sir Walter Lawrence, the resident commissioner of Kashmir at the turn of the last century, as a lake par excellence, it is surrounded by majestic snow-capped mountains. Much of the lake is a labyrinthine maze of intricate waterways. The lake is divided by causeways into four parts – Gagribal, Lokut Dal, Bod Dal and Nagin. Two small islands, known as the Char Chinar, are popular picnic spots, while along the lake lie the famous Mughal gardens and beautiful orchards. Chashme Shahi (the 'Royal Spring'), is the smallest of Srinagar's Mughal gardens with three terraces in addition to a natural spring enclosed in a stone pavilion.

Located just above the Chashme Shahi are the ruins of an astronomical observatory built by Dara Shikoh, the favourite son

Top: Trees lining a bank of the Dal lake in autumn.

Facing page (top): A view of the 14th-century Shah Hamadan mosque in Srinagar, built entirely of wood.

Facing page (centre): Zaina Kadal, one of the nine old bridges connecting the two banks of the Jhelum river flowing through Srinagar.

Facing page (bottom): The bubbling stream of the Sind river that flows through the Sonmarg meadow, 2800 metres above sea level.

of Mughal emperor, Shah Jahan. The largest of the gardens is the Nishat ('The Garden of Spring'), built by Empress Nur Jahan's brother, Asaf Khan, with several terraces and a central water course. The third Mughal garden, Shalimar, was planted by Jehangir, whose love for Kashmir brought him here thirteen times, more than any other Mughal ruler. Shaded by magnificent chinar trees, the Shalimar has a series of stone pavilions with flowing water and beautifully laid out flower beds.

Across the Dal from Shalimar on the western shore of the lake is the mosque of Hazratbal, the only one of its kind architecturally in Kashmir. Made of white marble with a dome and a minaret, Hazratbal is the repository of the Moi-e-Muqqadas (sacred hair) of the Prophet Mohammed, exhibited to the public on certain days of the year.

The oldest and largest of mosques of Kashmir are also in Srinagar. Shah Hamadan Masjid, a wooden structure with fine papier mâché workmanship on its walls and ceilings, is the oldest, with five facets, each of which has five arches, signifying the five daily prayers offered to Allah. Jamia Masjid, another wooden mosque built in the Indo-Saracenic style, is the largest.

In the heart of the city rises the 304-metre-high Shankaracharya hill, also known as the Takht-e-Suleiman or the 'Throne of Solomon'. It offers a breathtaking view of the city, the valley and the Pir Panjal range. The Shiva Temple here, according to Kalhan, was constructed by Raja Gopadatya in 371 BC and is

the oldest shrine in Kashmir. On the northeastern side of the Dal is Hariparbat, another sacred hill. Atop the Hariparbat is a fort built between 1592 and 1598 by the Mughal emperor, Akbar. On the southern side of the fort is the shrine of Makhdum Sahib, which draws hundreds of pilgrims, and below it is the mosque of Akhund Mulla Shah built by Dara Shikoh.

A walk through the old city is perhaps the best way to get acquainted with Srinagar. You can spend hours exploring the markets and they offer a great opportunity to pick up souvenirs. Exquisite papier mâché items such as boxes, vases, and wooden artifacts made of walnut wood are a good buy. What are special are carpets, known for their highly intricate decorations and patterns, with a strong Persian influence. Also famous are the pashmina shawls made from the hair of the ibex.

Renowned for its lakes, Srinagar is a city that seems surrounded by gleaming water. A *shikara* ride on the Dal lake is a must for any visitor to Kashmir as is at least a night's stay on one of its well-equipped houseboats. The calm waters of the Manasbal

lake, about 5 kilometres long and 1.2 kilometres wide, attract birds by the hundreds and it is not without reason that it has often been described as a bird watcher's paradise. An enchanting glide in water is on the Manasbal lake on a *shikara*. Lotus flowers and roots, locally called *nadroo*, and water chestnuts grow in plenty in Manasbal and add a gentle beauty to the quiet prevalent here.

About 60 kilometres to the northwest of Srinagar is the Wular lake, the largest freshwater lake in Asia. The size of the lake can vary between 30 to 260 square kilometres, depending on the season. It was formed following tectonic activity and the Jhelum river feeds into the lake, which acts as a natural flood reservoir. Before getting under the spell of the lake, it is advisable to visit Watlab with its shrine of a Muslim mystic, Baba Shukuruddin, high on a hilltop. From here, the Wular lake stretches away as far as the eye can see, with picturesque villages and emerald-green tilled fields ringing its banks.

Fish abound in the Wular lake, offering sustenance to thousands of people living in and around the lake, with more

than 8,000 fishermen earning their livelihood from it. The banks are a bird lover's delight, with the abundant bird life here – sparrow hawks, short-toed eagles, the Himalayan golden eagle, monal pheasant, chukar partridges, Kashmir rollers, Himalayan pied woodpeckers, and golden orioles, among many others.

Below left: A fountain at Chashme Shahi, or the 'Royal Spring', one of the three main Mughal gardens in Srinagar, the other two being Shalimar and Nishat.

Below right: Skiers on the snow at Gulmarg, one of the best ski resorts in India.

Bottom: A *shikara* boatman huddles in his *pheran*, or long coat, as mist envelops the Dal lake.

THE UNKNOWN KASHMIR
AMARNATH

Above: A *sadhu* poses with his *trishul* (three-pointed staff) as he makes his way to the holy cave of Amarnath, the abode of Lord Shiva.

Right: The pilgrimage path to Amarnath cave (3900 metres), the 45-kilometre trek passing through high valleys and glaciers.

A trek to the famed Amarnath cave, 141 kilometres from Srinagar, is a defining experience. The Amarnath cave, dedicated to Lord Shiva (the Destroyer and one of the trinity of Hindu gods – the other two being Brahma, the Creator, and Vishnu, the Preserver) is a popular and much sought-after *yatra* or pilgrimage for a devout Hindu and a fascinating and arduous trek for an adventure lover. This pilgrimage or trek starts from Pahalgam, 96 kilometres from Srinagar. It is held in July-August for 45 days, coinciding with the Hindu holy month of Shravan. The cave is at an altitude of 3900 metres and it takes five to six days to complete the 45-kilometre trek from Pahalgam to Amarnath. Camps are organized en route for pilgrims to stay the night. Prior permission is needed from the government before making the pilgrimage as terrorist attacks have occurred during the *yatra*.

There is an interesting tale regarding the discovery of the holy cave. There was once a Muslim shepherd named Buta Malik who was given a sack of coal by a *sadhu* (holy man). Upon reaching home he discovered that the sack, in fact, contained gold. Overjoyed, Malik rushed back to look for the *sadhu* and thank him. But the *sadhu* had vanished and a cave had appeared on the spot of their meeting. Eventually, this became a place of pilgrimage for all believers. Even today, a percentage of the donations made by pilgrims is given to the descendants of Malik, and the remaining to the trust that manages the shrine.

The first day's trek of 15 kilometres takes one from Pahalgam to Chandanwari along the Lidder river, and is an easy walk through a thick coniferous forest. The scenery is enchanting, with excellent views of the Lidder valley and high mountain ranges ahead.

It is the next day that the walk becomes a bit tough. The second day's trek of 12 kilometres winds through to Sheshnag lake through spectacular landscape. This high-altitude lake lies in the shadow of a mountain with seven peaks resembling the head of a mythical snake (in Hindu mythology, Sheshnag is a snake with seven heads). Throughout the day, a bubbling stream

Top (left and right): Thousands of pilgrims complete the arduous trek to reach the entrance of the Amarnath cave to pray before the huge ice *lingam* (phallus) – a natural stalagmite formation.

Facing page: A towering snow-covered mountain peak emerges out of the clouds to catch the rays of the rising sun on the way to the Amarnath cave.

is never far off from the track in a landscape that is untouched by the modern world. The overnight camp is on the shores of the beautiful lake that has still, deep blue waters.

The third day's 12-kilometre trek is the toughest and touches the highest point of the pilgrimage. The track winds up, gaining height metre by metre and when one reaches Mahagunas Pass, it is 4600 metres above sea level. The path then descends to reach a meadow and the last camp at Panchtarni.

The holy Amarnath cave is 6 kilometres from here and an early start is recommended for there is a long queue for entry to the cave. Inside the cave is the ice Shiva Linga (along with two other ice formations representing Lord Shiva's wife Parvati and his son Ganesh), a natural formation of an ice stalagmite in the form of *lingam* (phallus). This *lingam* grows and shrinks with the phases of the moon, reaching its height during the holiest day (decided by the Hindu calendar) of the pilgrimage. Legend has it that Lord Shiva recounted to Parvati the secret of creation here in the cave in Amarnath. Unknown to them, a pair of mating doves eavesdropped on this conversation and having learned the secret, are reborn again and again, with the cave as their eternal abode. Sighting the pair of doves is taken as a good sign by pilgrims, who believe that it is the same pair of doves that overheard the gods.

One has to return the same day to spend the night at Panchtarni or continue up to Sheshnag lake for the night halt. There is yet another shorter but tougher route to the cave. It is via a place called Sonemarg, about 60 kilometres northeast of Srinagar on the Srinagar-Leh highway. About 15 kilometres from Sonemarg is Baltal, in the charming little valley in the foothills of Zojila Pass. Amarnath is just a day's trek from here but the track is very steep and needs great caution. Also, it involves crossing a number of snow bridges on the fast-flowing streams, but reaching it is a reward in itself, the serene beauty of the mountain peaks offering a respite for city-jangled nerves.

HIMACHAL
THE COMPLETE PANORAMA

Shimla, the Queen of the Hills, still bears the stamp of the British Raj in its bungalows and churches. But the hill station is also the gateway to the treeless and brown cold desert of Spiti, where the mountains seem to be made of sand and loose rock and where Buddhism survives in the ancient Tabo and Ki monasteries.

Preceding page 54: Chandratal, or the 'Moon Lake', lies on the border of Spiti and Lahaul, with its clear deep blue waters.

Preceding page 55: The chorten at the entrance of the Ki monastery is one of the most elaborate examples of prayer stones in Spiti.

Shimla is a pampered city. Right from the day in 1822 when the first European house – the Kennedy House – came up here in what was then a village, the British treated it as a special place and spared no effort in providing it with all its material needs, so much so that by 1864, it had become the summer capital of the British empire.

Much before being declared the summer capital (and summer for the British meant April to October, the better part of the year), Shimla became a popular escape for the British. By the late 1830s, it had garnered a reputation as one of the most expensive cities in India, where 'the servants are bad and difficult to get.' By the early 1840s, there were complaints of it becoming too crowded. Bungalows were coming up fast in the area that the British had bought from the Maharaja of Patiala and Rana of Keonthal in the Shimla hills, but not fast enough to cater to the increasing number of visitors. Some British soldiers alluded to this by calling it 'Mount Olympus'.

Left: A view of the city of Shimla, the former summer capital of the British empire, built on seven hills.

Top: A trident post at the Dhankar monastery bears strings of prayer flags. The trident is a symbol of power in Tibetan Buddhism.

The reason for the rush was the climate. Even as the plains below burned in the heat of May, Shimla remained cool and breezy. The mean altitude of 2200 metres, coupled with the thick forest of cedar, pines and oak, kept the temperature under check. The construction boom continued in Shimla for this reason and because the initiative was all individual, a wide variety of architectural styles from Europe and India was used here – from Gothic to Victorian to Swiss to Tudor to local, alongwith an interesting mix of all.

When India got its Independence in 1947, Shimla became the capital of the Punjab province before becoming the capital of the new state of Himachal Pradesh in 1967. From being a small village to becoming a state capital with no in-betweens, it was small wonder that Shimla earned the sobriquet: 'The Queen of the Hills'.

It is this heritage that makes Shimla an interesting city to visit. It is a city made for walking and exploring the various architectural styles that it showcases. The Mall Road is the hub of Shimla and a shopping street that once was spoken of in the same breath as Paris and St. Petersburg. Even today, it retains its charm of being a traffic-free shopping area. The Scandal Point on the Ridge lies almost at the centre of Mall Road and can be the point to begin the heritage walks in Shimla. It got its name because of its location. Being the central point of the Mall Road, people gathered here and exchanged news and gossip that would have included the latest scandals. To its left are the Town Hall, the dressed-stone building built by the British which today houses the Municipal Corporation offices, and Gaiety Theatre, which was built in 1887 and is known for its fine acoustics, and has been the cultural hub of Shimla till date.

The journey from Shimla to Spiti valley, a cold desert region nearly 415 kilometres from Shimla and at a mean altitude of 3200 metres, is an experience to remember. When one starts from the green Shivaliks of Shimla it is difficult to imagine that the road will lead to a land where brown is the most dominant colour. From the wooded lower hills to the cold high deserts of Spiti, the road passes through the whole gamut of the Himalayan panorama.

The hills in and around Shimla are under the regime of the conifers – cedars, pines and firs. Oaks and rhododendrons accompany them, as they do in the rest of the Himalayas. It is

Top: Tourists flock to the Ridge at Shimla after a fresh snowfall. Shimla attracts thousands of visitors all round the year.

Facing page (top): The Christ Church is the most prominent building on the Mall Road of Shimla and is said to be the second oldest church in northern India.

Facing page (below): A blanket of snow covers the streets of Shimla, surrounded by spectacular mountains.

green all around and the ride from Shimla to Narkanda – 90 kilometres away – is a visual delight. More so, as the highway – the famous Hindustan-Tibet road – snakes through the spine of the ranges and it provides an excellent vantage point for views into the valleys flanking the route.

From Narkanda, a tourist hotspot because of its scenic beauty and thick forest cover, the road takes a plunge to meet the narrow valley of the aggressive Sutlej river. The mountains too change their character. The slopes are steep and the façade stern. The trees thin out and grasses take over. Rampur Bushair, 120 kilometres from Shimla, is the first town the road cuts through along the Sutlej. It is an old town, a former capital of the region. It has a vibrant bazaar, once the main one where traders from different valleys and from as far as Tibet converged to barter their goods. Even today that spirit seems alive here though the mix of goods has become more modern. In fact, if you visit it during the Lavi fair here in November, with a little imagination you could transport yourself to the times of yore. Traditional dances are held during the fair, where you will find local textile products, agricultural produce, and items for daily use.

It is here that the Hindu and Buddhist worlds first meet. Rampur Bushair is the gateway to the Kinnaur region of Himachal

60

Above: The Kinner Kailash ranges are almost at a touching distance from Kalpa, the former capital of Himachal's Kinnaur district.

Facing page (bottom): Multiple strings of prayer-flags flutter in the strong wind at Kunzum La, the pass between Spiti and Lahaul.

Pradesh that borders Tibet. The Tibetan influence can be seen on the architecture here. The quaint old parts of the huge royal palace – the Padam Palace with its wooden outhouses built in traditional style towers over the main road – and an 8th century Narasimha temple with fascinating stone carvings and statues that speak of its antiquity, are examples of this mixing of cultures.

From here on, the road follows the Sutlej, one of the fastest flowing rivers in Asia. It cuts though the steep mountainside rising above the Sutlej to meet it again at Wangtoo, the entry point to Kinnaur, the tribal district of Himachal Pradesh. A hop, skip and jump brings you to Recong Peo, the district headquarters, 260 kilometres from Shimla. Above it lies the earlier headquarters, Kalpa, situated on a spectacular spot. It faces the majestic Kinner Kailash peak (6350 metres) and the snowfields are so near that it seems you can extend your hand and touch them. So harsh is the climate here that it was one of the reasons that forced the authorities to move downhill and build the new township of Recong Peo.

You are now ready to make that final climb across into the Himalayas. But even then, the road ahead takes the first-time visitor by surprise. It crosses the Sutlej at a place called Khab – just a bridge on the river and a few tea shops – and then in spectacular, consecutive loops rises up the mountainside. Called the Ka loops (after the village of the same name that lies at the top), within 11 kilometres these propel you up into a landscape that is totally different from what you had encountered till now. There are no trees and the mountains seem to be made of just sand and rock.

THE UNKNOWN HIMACHAL
SPITI

The cold desert has begun and when you reach Sumdo (meaning 'where three mountain ranges meet'; you will come across many Sumdos in the cold desert regions of Spiti, Lahaul and Ladakh), you are in Spiti. The name 'Spiti' means 'Middle Country' – it lies between Tibet, Ladakh, Kinnaur, Lahaul and Kulu. Spiti is also the name of the main river of the region that starts from Kunzum La, a 4590-metre-high pass at the other end of the valley, and meets Sutlej near Khab. The average altitude of the Spiti valley is around 3200 metres with the lowest point at Sumdo and the highest towards Kunzum La. So, when you enter Spiti from Sumdo, you gain in altitude as you move ahead.

Right: Highly eroded column formations in Sarchu village, Spiti.

The first thing that strikes one when one reaches Spiti is the landscape. Treeless, the mountains seem to be made of sand and loose rock. Brown, and all its possible hues, is the dominant colour here with the Spiti river providing a lone thread of contrast. It is this vast aridness of the region at such an altitude that makes the view awe-inspiring. The landscape has the raw beauty of nature untrammelled by human hand and wild to the extreme. This land of sand and snow is like the Tibetan landscape, harsh but alluring. Some willow and poplar plantation has been done at some stretches along the road, but in view of the enormousness of the landscape, they seem to be just an exercise in tokenism. Here is an abrupt change in architecture – the houses are mostly made of mud and are flat-roofed. The reason: though the region is at a higher altitude than Kinnaur, the fact that it is in the shadow of the Great Himalayan ranges means that precipitation is much lower here, almost negligible.

There's yet another interesting spin-off of this cold desert landscape. It is quite difficult to estimate distances – with no landmarks as such and thus no point of reference, the distance always turns out to be much more than what one estimates. If you plan to trek here, this is important to remember.

Top left: Walking on a glacier in Spiti valley.

Left: Buddhist monks play drums and cymbals in Kungri monastery in Spiti's Pin valley.

Above: Colourful entrance gate to the town of Kaza in Spiti.

Left: The entrance to the Kaza monastery is protected by paintings of guardian deities. Virupaksha, the guardian of the west, has a red face and holds a serpent and stupa in his hands; Vaishrava, the guardian of the north, is yellow in colour and carries a banner of victory and a mongoose in his hands.

Below: The flat expanse of Kunzum La, which literally means 'Meeting Place of the Ibex'.

THE UNKNOWN HIMACHAL
TABO

Above: The Tabo monastery as seen from the old chortens in the monastery complex, which has nine temples, twenty-three chortens and a monk's chamber.

Right: A Buddhist monk is immersed in his prayers near the Tabo monastery, in Spiti.

After Sumdo, the first major stopover is Tabo. Known as the Ajanta of the Himalayas, the over thousand-year-old monastery, said to be second in importance only to the Tholing monastery in Tibet, is well worth a visit. The monastery has two parts – the old and the new. The old part is made purely of mud and the interiors are small and dark. The smell of yak butter burnt in prayer hangs here like a thick curtain. The new monastery was built incorporating parts of the old one.

As you enter the brilliantly whitewashed monastery, you see the wall paintings. Awash in brilliant colours – red, gold, silver, blues and magentas – the frescos hit you with an unprecedented force. It is a virtual riot of colours here amidst the purely browns outside. The monastery houses a priceless collection of manuscripts and *thangka*s (Buddhist scroll paintings), statues, frescos and murals depicting tales from the Mahayana Buddhist pantheon. Every inch of the wall is covered with fine paintings in astonishingly well-preserved condition. Nearly thirty-six, almost life-size clay statues, perch on the walls of the assembly hall. Above the monastery and across the road on small cliffs, there are a series of caves which were once used as dwelling units by the monks.

A few kilometres ahead of Tabo is a village called Shichling. From Shichling a small road cuts up the hill to reach Dhankar, the former capital of Spiti. Nestling at an altitude of 3870 metres is the thousand-year-old citadel of Dhankar. Strategically built on a spindle-like spur, the citadel allowed the Spitian in earlier times to keep vigil on the approaches and alert the people in case of danger. In fact, Dhankar means a safe sanctuary of rocks. The fort also has a notorious reputation. Its prison, which Nono (title for the king of Spiti) built sometime in the medieval period, is like a dungeon with just one opening at the top.

On the southern part of the slope stands an old monastery, founded between the 7th and the 9th centuries. It consists of a number of buildings perched together, giving a fortress-like impression. One of the major attractions of the Dhankar

Top left: A sanctuary in the Assembly Hall in Tabo. Lit by an opening in the roof, it houses stucco images of the venerated Amitabha attended by lesser deities.

Top right: The town of Tabo standing on a narrow stretch of the Spiti valley, where mountains shelter it from high winds.

monastery is a statue of Vairochana (Dhyan Buddha) consisting of four figures seated back to back. It also houses a collection of crumbling, but interesting *thangka*s. A freshwater lake lies about 3 kilometres above the village at a height of 4000 metres. Set amidst lush green pastures, the lake offers a perfect idyllic camping site. Some boating facilities are also proposed to be introduced in the near future.

Just after Shichling, while going to Kaza, headquarters of the Spiti sub-division of Lahaul and Spiti district, is a bridge to the left across the Spiti river. A big board announces: 'Welcome to Pin Valley, the home of Snow Leopard and Ibex'. If you are lucky – and chances of getting lucky are more just after winter in March-April – you might spot a herd of the impressive ibex, although the snow leopard is comparatively difficult to see. The Pin valley, named after the Pin river that flows through it, has yet another distinction – it is greener than the Spiti valley. It also has Spiti's second oldest monastery at Kungri. It provides unmistakable evidence of tantric cult as practised in Buddhism. It is the main centre of the Nyingmapa sect in Spiti, and perhaps the only branch of Buddhism in which use of weapons is practised. Nyingmapa is the oldest sect in Tibetan Buddhism and its followers are also known as Red Hats because of red monk hats that they wear.

Below and bottom: The centuries-old mud buildings and chortens in the old part of the Tabo monastery, also known as the Ajanta of the Himalayas.

THE UNKNOWN HIMACHAL
KI

Above: A monk dressed in traditional style during the Kalachakra ceremony in the presence of the Dalai Lama at the Ki monastery in the Spiti valley.

Right: Ki, the largest monastery in the Spiti valley, dominates its most populous part around Kaza.

Kaza is a big town compared to Tabo and Dhankar. It also has a monastery but its importance lies in the fact that it has a big bazaar where you can buy virtually anything of daily use. Also, it is the most populous town (the total population of Spiti is 10,679 according to the 2001 census, and nearly 3000 people live in Kaza), justifying its status as being the headquarters of Spiti. Overlooking Kaza from a height of about 4000 metres is the Ki monastery, 12 kilometres away. It is the largest in the valley and when seen from afar it looks amazingly like a honeycomb. It has irregular prayer chambers, interconnected by dark passages, tortuous staircases and small doors.

It is also known for its beautiful murals, *thangka*s, rare manuscripts, stucco images and peculiar wind instruments that form part of the orchestra whenever Chham (a dance performed by monks) is enacted here in summer. It has beautiful scriptures and paintings of the Buddha and other deities. Another interesting aspect of the monastery is its collection of weapons, a pointer to a more violent past when the monastery had to ward off marauders.

Above Ki is Kibber, a small village at a height of about 4300 metres. It is a pleasant village with lush green fields, much in contrast to the arid hills. Interestingly, the houses here are made of stone instead of mud, which is used extensively in the valley.

From Kaza to Kunzum La is a journey through desolation. The geological formations here have to be seen to be believed and are also a lesson in how colourful the seemingly drab can be. The

mountains here vary from being brilliant yellow in colour to vivid purple. Apart from a couple of small villages, the only place of note is Losar (it has a government guest house for visitors), at the foot of the Kunzum La, which forms the border between Spiti and Lahaul. The pass is awash with prayer flags and there is a temple at the top dedicated to Goddess Durga, besides a couple of chortens. The view from the top is breathtaking. On one side is the Spiti valley and on the other are numerous peaks of the Chandra-Bhaga range. From the pass, one can trek to the beautiful Chandratal, the 'Moon Lake'. Attracting thousands of visitors during the season, it surely deserves its reputation as being the most beautiful lake in the Himalayas. From Kunzum La, one can reach Manali in half a day via the Rohtang Pass. From Manali to Shimla is a day's journey.

Facing page: Chandratal lake, at an altitude of 4300 metres, is about three kilometres long and a kilometre at its widest part.

Top: The honeycomb structure of the Ki monastery on the banks of the Spiti river.

Above: Pilgrims arriving at the Ki monastery to take part in the Kalachakra ceremony.

UTTARAKHAND

ABODE OF THE GODS

Winding roads lead to ancient pilgrimage spots, temple towns, the sacred Ganga river, lofty mountains and thick forests in Uttarakhand, pausing at intriguing remote places such as the icy Roopkund lake, with its skeletal relics, and the ancient temples of Bageshwar and Jageshwar.

Preceding page 74: A waterfall at Suryakund near Gangotri, the seat of Goddess Ganga.

Preceding page 75: A *sadhu* immersed in prayers while sitting at the banks of the Bhagirathi river that originates from Gaumukh.

Though it is a state less than a decade old, Uttarakhand, carved from the state of Uttar Pradesh in November 2003 after a sustained campaign by the hill people for a state of their own, is a centuries-old mosaic of Indian culture and customs. The first mention of Uttarakhand (literally, the 'northern section'), with its pilgrimage centres, appears in the *Skanda Purana* and *Mahabharata* as Kedarkhand. For millennia, this region has been identified as the land of perpetual snow and the abode of gods where nature and divinity exist together, and where mountains and rivers are sacred, steeped in mythology.

Among the rivers of India, the Ganga (or the Ganges) is revered as the holiest. It is repeatedly invoked in the *Vedas*, the *Puranas*, and the two great Indian epics, the *Ramayana* and the *Mahabharata*. In Hindu mythology, the Ganga is not just a river, but a goddess, one of the two daughters of Meru or the Himalaya. According to mythology, this celestial river descended to earth as a result of penance done by King Bhagirath of the Ikshvaku dynasty to revive the souls of King Sagara's sixty thousand sons who had been burnt to ashes by the sage, Kapil. To help soften

Facing page: The massive Gangotri glacier, which is 30 kilometres long and 2–4 kilometres wide, with the twin peaks of Bhagirathi in the background.

Top: A *sadhu* poses with his sword and trident at a temple near the banks of the Ganga in Haridwar.

the impact of Ganga's descent to earth, Lord Shiva received the river in his matted locks and it is on the site of her descent that the present-day temple at Gangotri stands. Many other such tales are associated with the river and the Ganga has been described by Mahatma Gandhi as 'the river of India, beloved of her people, round which is intertwined her memories, her hopes and fears, her songs of triumph, her victories and her defeats. She has been a symbol of India's age-long culture and civilization, ever changing, ever flowing, and yet ever the same Ganges.'

The Ganga enters the plains of north India at Haridwar, located 214 kilometres northeast of Delhi in the foothills of the Shivalik hills. Haridwar is also known as Mayapuri, Gangadwara, Tapovan and Mokshadwar in ancient scriptures, a pilgrimage site held in reverence for centuries. It also finds mention in the travels of the Chinese pilgrim Huien Tsang, who visited India in the first millennium AD. This temple town is the first stop on the trail to the Himalayan pilgrimage shrines of Badrinath and Kedarnath, and is also where the festivities of the Kumbh Mela are held once in twelve years. The Kumbh Mela in Hindu mythology refers to the retrieval of the *amritkalasha*, or pot of nectar, from the *samudramanthan*, or churning of the ocean. In the fight for possession of this nectar between the gods and the demons, a few drops of nectar fell at four places: Prayag (Allahabad), Haridwar, Nasik and Ujjain. The Kumbh Mela commemorates this holy event, and this is when Hindus from all over the country come together to take a holy dip in the Ganga. The astrological date for the Kumbh Mela at Haridwar falls at the time when Venus and Jupiter coincide with Aquarius and the Sun enters Aries.

The five sacred *ghat*s or bathing spots in Haridwar are Gangadwara, Kankhal, Nila Parvata, Bilwa Teertha and Kusavarta. The main *ghat* at Haridwar is known as Hari-ki-Pauri (a footprint of Vishnu on a stone). Close by is the Gangadwara temple, the most visited temple here because of its religious significance – Haridwar was initially known as Gangadwara, the place where the holy Ganges leaves the Himalayas and enters the plains. Every evening, the bathing *ghat*s come alive with the sound of the Ganga *aarti* (prayer ceremony), which takes place after sunset. Offerings of lamps and flowers are made to the river

A *sadhu* prays at the snout of the Gangotri glacier that terminates at Gaumukh, 18 kilometres from Gangotri.

at the end of the *aarti* and the sight of hundreds of miniature lamps floating along in the dark water has been described by many as a truly moving moment.

Moving northeast, less than 25 kilometres away from Haridwar, is yet another important stop on the banks of the Ganga – Rishikesh. At the confluence of the Chandrabhaga river and the Ganga, Rishikesh represents the site where Vishnu vanquished the demons Madhu and Kaitabha. It is also believed that Lord Rama's brother, Bharat, meditated here. The sage Raibhya Rishi is believed to have sat on the banks of the Ganga and performed such severe penance to please the gods that he was rewarded by Lord Vishnu, who appeared before him in the form of Rishikesh. This is how the place got its present name (which means 'holy man's locks'). Over the ages, saints have meditated at this peaceful spot, and it has been the stepping stone to the holy shrines and sites stretching across the lofty Himalayas – Badrinath, Kedarnath, Gangotri, and Yamnotri.

In the mornings, people come down to the river to bathe and pray. At dusk, like in Haridwar, the *aarti* on the Triveni Ghat here is an unforgettable experience. Scores of devotees sit in rows on the steps of the *ghat* and as the sun begins to set, infusing the river with its golden orange hue, priests hold plates of flaming clarified butter, moving them in circular salutation to the river

Ganga. Flower-filled leaf boats carrying tiny oil lamps are released and allowed to float on the river, lighting the night in an almost ethereal glow. The entire ceremony of worship reverberates in remembrance and faith.

The river can be crossed over the two bridges that span it: the Lakshman Jhula, a 137-metre-long suspension bridge built in 1939 as a hanging jute (rope) bridge, and Ram Jhula. The road leading to the Lakshman Jhula entrance is lined with stalls selling trinkets, lemonade, incense, offerings and other items. The bridge itself is very crowded as pedestrians, motorbikes and cows jostle with each other on their way across it. The Ram Jhula is the newer of the two bridges.

Once the bridges are crossed, the towering Trymbakeshwar temple can be seen on the far bank. This huge temple has thirteen levels and devotees can be seen working their way up the stairs and corridors, every pilgrim ringing a bell as each level is reached. A temple to Lakshmana, brother of Lord Rama, is situated on the opposite bank of the Ganga in a serene place called Tapovan. According to legend, Lakshman carried out penance here.

From here, we follow the Ganga to Devprayag, which marks the confluence of the two mighty Himalayan rivers, the Bhagirathi and the Alaknanda, which together give rise to the Ganga. The Bhagirathi, regarded as the source of the Ganga, rises in the

Top left: The Ganga temple at Gangotri, one of the four major pilgrimage sites in the Garhwal Himalayas.

Top right: The 18-kilometre trek from Gangotri to Gaumukh is dotted with a number of places of worship.

snow-swept ranges at Gaumukh, and it is at this stage that we have to part with the Ganga at Rishikesh on our way to the source. From Rishikesh to the temple town of Gangotri is about 248 kilometres, with numerous charming places on the route such as Narendra Nagar, Tehri, Dharasu, Makuri, Uttarkashi, Gangnani, Sukhi and Bhaironghati.

Narendra Nagar was built by the king of Tehri, Narendra Singh. The royal palace here is worth seeing for its grandeur as is the magnificent statue of Lord Shiva's attendant, the Nandi bull. Tehri is the site of the famous Tehri dam. For all intents and purposes, the old town of Tehri is now history. All one can see of the 200-year-old town is the historic Clock Tower, built in 1887 in memory of Queen Victoria, as well as a few remnants of the Old Durbar, the seat of the Tehri kingdom, but even this is possible only when the water level is down.

Uttarkashi is a pilgrimage centre of great importance. The main temple in the town is that of Vishwanath, flanked by the temples of Durga and Hanuman. Bhaironghati, an overgrown village, lies in a picturesque forested area, where a small temple of Bhairon, appointed by Shiva to safeguard this region, stands. The bridge over the Jhanvi river at Bhaironghati is said to be the highest in Asia and the view of the river gorge is an experience in itself.

Less than 10 kilometres away from this spot is Gangotri, the name meaning 'the descent of the Ganges'. A shrine dedicated to the goddess was built here about 250 years ago by Amar Bahadur Thapa, a Gorkha commander. Near the temple is a great stone slab, the 'Bhagirath Shila' dedicated to Bhagirath, whose penance is believed to have brought the Ganga down from the heavens. Gangotri also marks the confluence of the Bhagirathi with Kedar Ganga. Gaumukh, the source of Bhagirathi, is 18 kilometres away from here.

The boulder-strewn valley of the Gaumukh glacier is ringed by high peaks. The peaks of Bhagirathi I and Bhagirathi II can be seen here.

THE UNKNOWN UTTARAKHAND
ROOPKUND

Above: A view of the snow-capped peaks from Kasauni, a small hill station in the Kumaon hills.

Right: The holy Trishul Peak as seen from a ridge just above the Roopkund lake, also called the 'Lake of Mysteries'.

On the way back from Gaumukh, a fascinating sight is the 'mystery lake' called Roopkund. The lake is located at an altitude of 5029 metres at the base of the Trishul peak in Chamoli district. Roopkund gained the sobriquet of 'The Mystery Lake' following the accidental discovery in 1942 of hundreds of human skeletons around the lake and on the lakebed. The skeletons are clearly visible through the waters during the brief one-month when the ice melts. In 2004, specimens of these skeletal remains, some with bits of flesh attached to them, were collected by a team from the National Geographic channel and taken to the Centre for Cellular and Molecular Biology at Hyderabad for detailed DNA tests.

There are a number of theories about the presence of these skeletons in the uninhabitable icy wastes of the Himalayas. Popular among these are that the skeletons are remains of soldiers or of pilgrims caught in a snowstorm, to the more fanciful theory which links the ancient remains to the Pandavas. Though the results from Hyderabad are only preliminary, it has been proved that the skeletal remains are of men, women and children of Indian origin who perhaps belonged to one family since the DNA of some skeletons matched each other. The skeletons are of tall people and have the distinguishing feature of an extra bone in their skulls, a rare feature which can help identify the probable population group.

The trek to Roopkund starts at Loharjung (height 2600 metres), on the Gwaldam-Karanprayag road, a tiny pass that is a gateway to the Wan valley, the last village on the trek to Roopkund. It is the last point to replenish supplies for the trek and to hire a guide, porters and mules. The trek to Roopkund needs to be spaced out depending upon the physical conditioning and experience of the trekkers. Most treks to Roopkund and back are six- to eight-day treks. The first section of the trek is from Loharjung to Didna, a five-hour gentle trek to the camping site at

Above: Visitors throng to catch a glimpse of the glacial Roopkund lake and the skeletal remains visible on its shores when the ice melts.

Facing page: Clouds part to give a glimpse of the 7817-metre-high Nanda Devi Peak, the second highest peak in India.

Didna, a meadow located above Kulling village. Didna to Bedni Bugyal (via Ali Bugyal) is a five- to six-hour trek, which starts off as a steep climb and ends in a gentle walk. At an elevation of 3500 metres, the campsite at Bedni Bugyal is perhaps one of the best camping sites in the Garhwal Himalayas. It is a green meadow and is profusely covered by a rich tapestry of alpine flowers after the rains. There is a small lake situated at the centre of the meadow, while close by is a temple where pilgrims offer prayers.

Bedni Bugyal to Bhagwabasa is a four- to five-hour trek and varies from a comfortable ascent at the beginning, to a gradual descent with a stiff climb in the middle of the route, and ends in an easy walk. The final stage is the walk from Kalu Vinayak, above the snow line, to Bhagwabasa, a cluster of stone huts put up by locals turned entrepreneurs. The final section of the trek is from Bhagwabasa to Roopkund, which can be done in about three hours and is graded as moderate to difficult. The trick is to make an early start in the morning, while the snow is still crunchy and easier to walk on. More often than not, most trekkers turn back because the snow starts to melt and makes it twice as difficult to climb because of the slipperiness.

The Roopkund lake is technically a tarn, or a glacier lake, formed by erosion over the centuries in an amphitheatre-like valley at the head of a glacier. This lake, which remains frozen for most part of the year, has an aura of mystique that is almost eerie. It is surrounded by imposing rock-strewn glaciers and impressive snow-clad peaks. The peaks, which can be seen from here and from Junargali, include the awe-inspiring Nanda Devi (7817 metres), Trishul (7120 metres) and the Nanda Ghunti (6390 metres). The best time to trek to Roopkund is from the end of August to the last week of October.

THE UNKNOWN UTTARAKHAND
BAGESHWAR
JAGESHWAR

From mystery to divinity is just a hop, skip and jump away. From Debal, the road continues to Gwaldam, at the edge of Chamoli district. Ahead of Gwaldam you enter into Bageshwar district of the Kumaon region. The peak of Nanda Devi, at 7817 metres the second highest peak in India, dominates the view all through this district. Nanda Devi is revered as a goddess and exerts great spiritual influence on the culture and life of the Kumaon region. An excellent spot from which to photograph the Nanda Devi range is the state bungalow at Kasauni, which is a serene hill station nestling on the hills overlooking the historic town of Bageshwar.

The road from Kasauni to Binsar passes through Bageshwar. Situated at the confluence of the Saryu, Gomti and Bageshwar rivers, it is intimately associated with Lord Sadashiva, the redeemer of all sins. The most important temple here is dedicated to Bagnath or Vyagreswar, the 'Tiger Lord', a form of Shiva. The temple was erected during the reign of the Kumaon king, Laxmi Chand, in the 15th century. The other important temple here is the Chandika temple. The Uttarayani fair, on the occasion of Makar Sankranti in January every year, attracts huge crowds of devotees to Bageshwar to bathe at the confluence of the Saryu and Gomti rivers. Bageshwar is also used as a base camp by trekkers for reaching the Pindari glacier. The other treks from Bageshwar are the routes to the Pindari-Kafni and Sundar-Dhunga glaciers.

From Bageshwar to Binsar, the road winds through some of the most beautiful sections of the Kumaon hills. Binsar is situated

Left: A thick forest of ancient cedars encircles the temple complex of Jageshwar in the narrow Jata Ganga valley.

Facing page: An exquisitely carved statue at an old temple in Bageshwar, which is associated with Lord Sadashiva, the redeemer of all sins.

in the middle of a forest reserve known as the 'Binsar Reserve', now a wildlife sanctuary. Binsar takes its name from the presiding deity of Lord Vineshwara in the temple here. Ruled by the Katyuri dynasty and then by the 'Chand' kings who ruled Kumaon up to 1790, Binsar later caught the fancy of the British (it finds a mention in the Atkinson's *Gazetteer* of the 1800s), who established estates and farms here.

Binsar is closely associated with Lieutenant General Sir Henry Ramsay, a cousin of Lord Dalhousie, the Viceroy of India. Ramsay, popularly known as the 'Uncrowned King of Kumaon', was so enchanted with the beauty of Binsar that he decided to settle here in a stretch of beautiful land amid hills, now known as the 'Binsar Estate'.

The Binsar Wildlife Sanctuary has been created for the conservation and protection of the shrinking broad-leaf oak forests of the central Himalayan region. Spread over an area less than 50 square kilometres, the sanctuary is rich in both flora and fauna. With over 200 species of birds, it is high on the list of bird-watching enthusiasts. Perched atop the Jhandi Dhar hills, it offers an untrammelled view of the Himalayas, with a 300-kilometre stretch of famous peaks, including Kedarnath, Chaukhamba, Trishul, Nanda Devi, Nanda Kot and Panchchuli.

Less than half-an-hour away from Binsar is Jageshwar. It lies in the narrow Jata Ganga valley, thickly forested with huge, ancient deodars. Considered to be among the twelve *jyotirlinga*s, Jageshwar was one of the sites chosen by the Katyuri rulers and later by the 'Chand' kings to construct temples. The temple complex here has about 164 temples built in honour of Lord Shiva, though it is said that there were once over 400 temples here. The temple complex is set amidst tall deodar trees with the Jata Ganga river flowing past. The three outstanding shrines here are dedicated to Jageshwar, Mrityunjaya (forms of Lord Shiva) and Pushtidevi (a manifestation of Goddess Durga). The Mahamrityunjaya temple is believed to be the oldest of all the temples and dates back to the 8th century AD. At this temple the Mahamrityunjaya *jaap* (mantra) is chanted, for a price, by a group of 718 pundits who recite it by rotation, 100,001 times. And as you listen to the monotonous chanting and gaze at the forests, river, and valley slopes, you are left with the powerful feeling of being in communion with nature and its divine spirit.

Above: The Dandeshwar temple in Jageshwar, one of the twelve *jyotirlinga*s in India. *Jyotirlinga*s are the most revered sites in the country where Lord Shiva is worshipped.

Facing page: Binsar, situated atop the Jhandi Dhar hills in Kumaon, provides a ringside view of the high peaks of Garhwal.

NEPAL
THE HEART OF THE HIMALAYAS

Surrounded by the mightiest peaks in the world, Nepal offers a glimpse into Buddhist and Hindu traditions and some of the most rewarding trekking trails. It is home to the hidden valley of Humla and the desolate landscape of Dolpo, which have remained closed to the outside world for centuries.

S tretching across Nepal from the eastern to the western edge, the Himalayas are at their most majestic here, with some of the world's highest peaks vying with one another for supremacy.

Nepal, a small landlocked country, boasts of a widely diverse landscape – eight of the top ten highest mountains in the world, snowy slopes that beckon skiers, thick jungles, and valleys that invite safaris and treks.

Buddhist and Hindu cultures provide a colourful and fascinating mix of people, lifestyles and festivals, an experience that begins with a visit to Kathmandu, the capital. The terrain of Kathmandu is a steep incline, descending from the Himalayan heights to the Terai flatland within a short distance. This mesmerizing city is believed to have more temples than houses and its festival calendar exceeds the number of days in a year.

Preceding page 90: The peak of Ama Dablam, 6812 metres high, towers over an old stupa in the Nepal Himalayas.

Preceding page 91: A shaman in Humla valley invokes the gods.

Left: A caravan of horses crosses a valley on a suspension foot-bridge over the Kali Gandaki river in the Annapurna region.

Top: The all-seeing eyes of Buddha on the Swayambunath stupa keep a watch on the Kathmandu valley. Perched atop a forested hill on the western edge of the valley, it is considered Kathmandu's most important Buddhist shrine.

Kathmandu is not only the administrative capital of the country but also the cultural capital of Nepal. Three Durbar Squares – Kathmandu, Patan and Bhaktapur – alongwith the temples of Pashupatinath, Bouddhanath, Swayambhunath and Changunarayan, are a favourite of visitors. The old city has a plethora of pagodas, narrow cobbled lanes, ancient carved windows, and stone shrines, all of which offer a peek into the historic and cultural past of the city.

A short distance outside Kathmandu, prayer flags and ceremonial bells greet the visitor at Gosainkund, a sacred lake. Hindu mythology relates how Lord Shiva took a dip in the lake to relieve the agonizing pain he suffered after swallowing poison to save the world. Adherents of the Hindu faith believe that if a person is immersed in the waters of Gosainkund and then pays a visit to Lord Shiva's temple, he or she will attain nirvana (enlightenment) with little effort. This belief has prompted thousands of pilgrims to visit Gosainkund during the religious festivals of Janai Purnima and Dashain.

Gosainkund, 4380 metres above sea level, is also a popular trekking destination that forms part of a number of trekking trails. One of the trails leaves from Dhunche, which is an eight-hour journey by bus from Kathmandu. The first climb here is up to Sing Gompa at a height of 3250 metres, after which trekkers tackle the steep climb to Gosainkund, which offers spectacular views of Ganesh Himal at 7130 metres. The lodges around the lake offer basic overnight facilities for a much-needed rest after the climb. Trekkers can then retrace their steps to Dhunche or continue to Tharepati and connect with the popular Helambu or Langtang routes through valleys and highland villages. In fact, to

Top: A view of the Durbar Square in Patan, encompassing the residence of the former royal family of Patan and a number of temples, all in the ancient Newari architectural style.

Above: A mountaineer in the Khumbu region enjoys the view of the setting sun on Mount Everest, the highest peak in the world.

avoid altitude sickness after the rapid ascent from Dhunche to Gosainkund, it is wiser to approach Gosainkund from the gentler Helambu and Langtang routes.

Spectacular, awe-inspiring, frightening, and dangerous are just some of the adjectives people have used to describe the world's highest mountain, Mount Everest. It continues to be the prime draw for people visiting Nepal, irrespective of whether they are die-hard mountaineers or mere amateurs. Treks to the Everest base camp, without actually attempting the summit, are becoming increasingly popular on both the north and south sides of the mountain. The climbers are a major source of revenue for the Nepalese government, which requires all prospective climbers to obtain an expensive permit, costing up to US $25,000 a person.

On the north side, the Rongbuk monastery stands at the foot of the Rongbuk glacier, beneath the Everest's massive north face. The monastery's location was selected specifically to allow religious contemplation of the great peak as was that of the Thyangboche monastery, set high on a ridge overlooking the Dudh Kosi river. Mount Everest, also known by the Tibetan name Chomolangma (Goddess Mother of the Snows), and by the Nepali name Sagarmatha (Mother of the Universe), looms ahead in all its might and mysteriousness, a regal divinity in itself. Close to it is the almost equally impressive Ama Dablam mountain.

Top: A view of the Annapurna ranges from Thulobugin ridge. Peaks seen here are (from left to right) Annapurna South, Fang, South Summit and Annapurna I, which soars to 8078 metres.

Right: Clouds frame a stone structure (typical in this region), at Kagbeni in northern Nepal.

It is the Annapurna Trail – one of the best walks in the world – that should not be missed. The route concentrates on the foothills of the mountain and the small villages along the way, making it a trek that is a discovery of people as much as it is about Himalayan landscapes. Also called the Annapurna Village Trek, the eighteen-day sojourn begins at 900 metres above sea level and reaches its highest point, the Thorung La pass, at about 5300 metres. The Annapurna region is well served by Pokhara, the main hub and staging post for the region northwest of the Kathmandu valley.

The tenth highest peak in the world, Annapurna (the name translates into 'Goddess of the Harvest' or 'The Provider') towers over the Kali Gandak river, with peaks on either side of its massif. These peaks are known as Annapurna I and Annapurna II. The main trekking route, the 300-kilometre Circuit Trek, comprises paths used in ancient times for trade between Tibet and Nepal,

and circles the majestic Annapurna. One is treated to spectacular views of the Annapurna and Dhaulagiri peaks and may even spot some of the teeming wildlife the region is known for. The advantage of a circuit is that there is no backtracking, so every day is a new experience, and an unforgettable one at that.

Top: The sunken bath of Tusha Hiti in Sundari Chowk is a part of the Patan Durbar Square. The Sundari Chowk also contains exquisite woodcarvings, and stone and metal sculpture.

Above: The Buddhist gompa at Tetang in Nepal's Mustang region is dwarfed by the highly eroded mountainsides, made up of one of the oldest sedimentary deposits in the Himalayas.

THE UNKNOWN NEPAL
HUMLA

Deep in the heart of the Himalayas, nestled between the Indian subcontinent and the Tibetan plateau, Humla lies hidden in the far northwest corner of Nepal. The towering Saipal range and the sacred Takh and Changla Himalayas loom over this barren forgotten basin of the mighty Karnali river, which originates from the Mansarovar lake region in Tibet. Humla's elevation varies between 1524 metres and 7337 metres. The natives speak an archaic dialect of Tibetan and Nepali languages. Summer in Humla is pleasant while the winter is harsh and cold, leaving the region isolated and mostly snowbound.

Though politically the region lies in Nepal, culturally it is closer to Tibet. The soul of Humla is the people and their culture. During the medieval period, the Humlis of the Karnali region,

Mani mask dancers at the Mani festival that marks the setting in of the spring season in Humla. The masked dances are a long-established part of Bonpo religious ceremonies.

were a powerful empire led by the potent Buddhist Dharma-Rajas. Today, they are a peaceful people, leading a simple, rural life in harmony with their environment. The wealth of flora and fauna here make Humla the home of many natural products of high value, while typical Humli handicrafts are slowly making their way into the market.

The lack of roads and difficult air access ensures Humla's distance from the rest of the world. With the border between Nepal and Tibet recently reopened, a great new trek is now possible. Beginning in Kathmandu, you can fly to Simikot, the capital of Humla district, and from there, trek north to Taklakot, in a path once taken by ancient Tibetan traders carrying caravan loads of salt for Nepalese buyers in exchange for grain. The climate changes from warm to well below freezing. At Taklakot, a jeep ride takes you to the base of Mount Kailash. From here, the pilgrim and tourist alike follow the *kora*, the trek around the revered mountain.

The extraordinarily beautiful and dramatic terrain of the Humla region is a delight for trekkers. But for the traditional trading tribe of Bhutias, who populate the lower Humla, Limi and upper Humla Karnali valleys, life here is stark and tough. The summer, the main agricultural season, is too short and the winter too long. Over centuries, forests have been cleared for firewood and for pine resin to fuel feeble lamps – the jharro (resin soaked pine wood) is used for cooking, and for providing light and heat in homes. However, it emits a thick black smoke that, in a confined area, causes acute respiratory ailments.

The best months to visit this area are between May and September. The weather is sunny and warm, although the nights are cold and temperatures can fall to below freezing. Weather can change rapidly and be unpredictable.

Also worth visiting in Humla is the remote Limi valley. It is at a high altitude and very narrow. There are three villages in the Limi valley that are immensely beautiful, rich in biodiversity, and steeped in ancient culture. These villages – Til, Halji and Jang – form the most remote areas of the Humla region and are the least developed. Limi valley is a six-day walk from Simikot.

Til is the westernmost of the three villages and is at an altitude of 3850 metres. It is approachable from Simikot via the Nyalu Pass, which is open between May and November. It is an extremely attractive village and is said to be one of the highest permanently inhabited places in Nepal. Some spectacular unnamed peaks are visible from here. Up the Til valley are creeks and birch forests, barley, wheat and potato fields and grazing areas. The nearest glacier is a mere 5 kilometres away, but it takes the better part of a whole day to reach there due to the rugged terrain and the high altitude.

Half-a-day's walk from Til is Halji village. This is the biggest village in Limi, located below a dramatic cliff with a hermitage clinging to it, and surrounded by high Limi peaks approaching 6000 metres. Up the side valley you enter a barren high valley leading over a pass into a plateau. On this plateau as well as on the higher regions is grazing land for Halji's herds of sheep, goats, horses and yaks and blue sheep abound in this region.

Two faces of Mani mask dancers in Humla – a jumping clown (*facing page*) performer leaping in the air, and a demon mask dancer (*right*), who is said to frighten the real demons away.

THE UNKNOWN NEPAL
DOLPO

Above: A man with a prayer wheel sitting on the stone steps
of his house, at Tsharka village in the Dolpo region.

Right: Fog sits amidst the green forested slopes of the Himalayas near
Chaurikot, in the Dolpo region of Nepal.

On the edge of the Tibetan plateau, north of the great mountain of Dhaulagiri, lies the remote and little-known land of Dolpo, a cold, arid region of bare rocky hills, narrow ravines and broad sparsely vegetated valleys. One of the last enclaves of pure Tibetan Buddhist culture, its spiritual centrepiece is Shey, the Crystal Mountain, a peak embedded with crystal deposits that shimmer in the sun, and Shey Gompa, the monastery at its base. Between 1530 and 1700, a number of small monasteries, such as Shey, Margom and Yang-tsher, were founded in Dolpo by visitors on a spiritual quest. Being in the Himalayan rain shadow, the area is unaffected by the monsoon rains. It is very dry and very hot in summer but, since much of the region is above 4000 metres, it is snow-covered and bitterly cold in winter.

Despite its inaccessibility, high altitude and inhospitable climate, Dolpo is not an empty land. It is an area of roughly 5500 square kilometres inside Nepal's northwestern frontier with Tibet, encompassing some thirty villages and monasteries at altitudes ranging from 3400 to 4500 metres. Walking through this land means walking through an ancient culture, one that has remained unchanged for thousands of years and is still almost untouched by the modern world; there are no motorized vehicles, or indeed machines, of any kind to be seen here. Living a marginal existence dependent on grain imports from the south, the few inhabitants of Dolpo cannot feed travellers, so trekkers in the area must be self-sufficient and carry enough stocks of food. Access to much of the area is restricted to only a few organized groups and strict environmental rules apply; everything carried in must be carried out to prevent the over-use and environmental damage that have arisen in other areas of Nepal.

The Dolpo-pa, as the people of Dolpo are called, are physically and culturally more Tibetan than Nepalese. The inhabitants are exclusively of the Tibetan stock and maintain strong links with Tibetan people through trade and cultural ties. Being totally cut off from the rest of the world for most part of the year, Dolpo is not an easy destination to reach, even in summer.

Today, Dolpo society is a study in old cultural norms. It is not feudal and the village elders have the authority to take

decisions for the village. Villages are small and far apart, isolated in deserted valleys. A village normally comprises a few stone houses surrounded by barley and buckwheat fields. The monasteries of Dolpo are the places of training and preparation for Dolpo's lamas, who spend many years in meditation and fulfil many roles, travelling widely in Dolpo, mediating disputes, teaching and using their skill as healers. In a culture with no judicial system, no schools and no health care system, the lamas thus have enormous influence.

The Dolpo region, one of the highest inhabited plateaus in the world, was closed to trekkers until 1989. Those who did get to visit this area needed special permission from the government. With the changes in the regulations governing visits, Dolpo has suddenly become a major destination for trekkers and mountain lovers. Lower Dolpo, the area opened to trekkers, is thickly forested with conifers and traversed by gushing rivers. The upper

portion of Dolpo, however, is an extension of the Tibetan plateau, with wild, windswept, open spaces characteristic of Tibet. The region was declared a National Park in 1984, making it Nepal's largest Park and the only one encompassing a trans-Himalayan ecosystem. The National Park status has helped preserve not only the culture but also wildlife. The lower Dolpo region is home to the endangered musk deer, which may be glimpsed along the trails, and to a great variety of birds. Though rarely seen, the blue sheep, the Himalayan black bear, snow leopard and the Himalayan wolf are also found in Dolpo.

The Dolpo is truly one of the most desolate places to live in. The inhabitants are in a few thousands and are entirely dependent on the small fields that they cultivate for barley and potatoes, but they have survived through the centuries, preserving their culture and tradition, and now allowing the outside world a glimpse of their age-old way of life.

Facing page: Ribbons and flowers decorate a wooden spirit effigy at a village in the Dolpo region.

Top: An ice and rock formation on a glacier in Nepal. This type of formation occurs when ice melts around a boulder.

TIBET
ROOFTOP OF THE WORLD

From Lhasa, the capital of Tibet, to the secret trails winding up the awe-inspiring Himalayas, every corner of Tibet is imbued with spirituality linked to the everyday lives of people. In this spiritual land are found such intriguing rituals as the practice of sky burials. Watching over Tibet is the majestic Mount Kailash, the 'Jewel of the Snows' that is its mystic soul.

erched on the high plateau of Central Asia and encircled by lofty mountains, Tibet is also referred to as the 'Roof of the World'. Stretching 2000 kilometres in length to 1000 kilometres in breadth, the plateau rises to over 4000 metres and then slopes down from the north towards the east where it meets the lowlands of the Chinese provinces of Sichuan and Yunnan. Tibet was annexed by China in 1959 and the Dalai Lama – the spiritual and temporal leader of Tibetans – and his entourage had to escape into exile in India. Today, it is known as the Tibet Autonomous Region and includes the Dalai Lama's former domain, consisting of Ü-Tsang and western Kham, while Amdo and eastern Kham are part of the Qinghai, Gansu, Yunnan, and Sichuan provinces of China.

'We turned a corner, and saw, gleaming in the distance, the golden roofs of the Potala, the most famous landmark of Lhasa ...' wrote Austrian mountaineer Heinrich Harrer in *Seven Years in Tibet*, an enthralling tale of his flight from an Indian prison to the Forbidden City, as Lhasa is called. Lhasa has for long figured on the wish list of travellers. Covered by a veil of secrecy and rendered unapproachable due to its remoteness and unhabitable terrain,

Left: A pilgrim looks at Mount Kailash that is considered sacred in four religions – Hinduism, Buddhism, Jainism and the Bon faith. For the Bon, the mountain is seen as indestructible, eternal and unchanging.

Above: A monk walks among the many buildings of Ganden monastery, 40 kilometres from Lhasa.

Lhasa had always been the lodestone for travellers seeking to unravel its mystique. A huge blank on the map of Asia in the 1800s, Tibet attracted not only explorers like Sven Hedin and Alexandra David-Neel but also surveyors (called 'pundits') from the Survey of India, sent by the British as part of a clandestine mission to fill out the blank on the map. Others were soon to follow, including Francis Younghusband, Francis Kingdon Ward and George Forrest, also explorers. The Forbidden City even today attracts its fair share of footprints. With the opening of the Qinghai-Tibet railway, Lhasa is now far more accessible than it ever was.

Girdled by high mountains, with their peaks soaring up to over 5500 metres, this ancient city overlooks the north bank of Kyichur river from a height of 3650 metres. In the Tibetan language, Lhasa means the 'Holy Land' and has been for centuries the hub of Tibet's politics, economy and culture.

Lhasa was designated as Tibet's capital city by Lobsang Gyatso, the fifth Dalai Lama, credited with instilling a sense of national unity in Tibet. He decided to build a palace on top of Marpo Ri or the Red Hill, the site of a ruined palace built by King Songtsen Gampo in AD 636 for his Nepalese wife. The foundations of the new palace were laid and work began in 1645. This palace was named after Mount Potala, the abode of Avalokiteshwara, who is regarded in Tibetan tradition as the founder and protector of the Tibetan race.

By 1649, the Potrang Karpo, or White Palace, was completed and the Dalai Lama and his government moved into it, while the Potrang Marpo, or Red Palace, was added between 1690 and 1694. The Potala's thirteen storeys, with sloping stone walls, contain over 1,000 rooms, 10,000 shrines and about 200,000 statues. The building measures 400 metres east-west and 350 metres north-south. It was the chief residence of the Dalai Lama until the fourteenth and present Dalai Lama was forced to flee Tibet in 1959. Today, the palace is a popular tourist attraction, and a UNESCO World Heritage Site.

A visit to the Potala Palace is sought after by visitors, but it is not as simple as it may seem. During the peak tourist season (May

to October), only a limited number of visitors are allowed to enter the palace on a daily basis, the tickets being garnered by travel agencies much in advance. However, it is possible to visit the former royal village at the foot of the castle instead. This is where the royal staff, guildsmen and high-ranking monks once lived and it is now an open-air museum, showcasing traditional Tibetan crafts, beautifully decorated interiors, cultural relics and several photo exhibitions about Tibet's transformation since the 1950s.

From Potala Square, a walk along Beijing Street, through the large commercial Chinese city-style shopping area, leads to the old inner city quarters, with its dense maze of alleys and tiny squares. The biggest square is the Barkhor Square, with the entrance to the Jokhang temple on its eastern side. The street that encircles Jokhang temple is actually the circumambulation path around the temple. The Jokhang Square is a hub of activity, from pilgrims prostrating themselves at every corner to tourists engaged in hectic parleying with vendors, and it is the ideal place to observe the religious practices, culture and economic dealings of Tibetans.

For Tibetans, pilgrimage is an important aspect one's life. It is the journey from ignorance to enlightenment, from self-centredness and materialistic preoccupations to a deep sense of the relativity and interconnectedness of all life. The Tibetan word for pilgrimage, *neykhor*, means 'to circle around a sacred place'. The goal of pilgrimage is not just to reach a particular destination but also to transcend, through travel, the attachments that restrict awareness of a larger reality.

The Jokhang temple, originally built during the reign of King Songsten Gampo, was first called the Tsulag Khang or 'House of Wisdom', but is now known as the Jokhang, which means the 'House of the Lord'. The story goes that Bhrikuti Devi, the daughter of the Nepalese King Amshuvarman, married King Songtsen Gampo in the 7th century AD, bringing an image of the Buddha with her to the Tibetan kingdom. Said to have been blessed by Lord Buddha himself, the image was considered sacred by Tibetans and a temple was built over a small lake, filled with logs and earth, to house it. This was the Jokhang

Facing page: A huge Buddha is painted on a rocky outcrop on the outskirts of Lhasa. Slightly smaller in size are paintings of other Tibetan Buddhist deities.

Above: Details of a painting at Jokhang temple in Lhasa. Jokhang temple was included as part of the Potala Palace in UNESCO's World Heritage list in 2000.

temple, venerated by Tibetans and a key destination of Buddhist pilgrimage for centuries. It was sacked several times by the Mongols, but the building survived. The original temple complex has undergone several accretions over the centuries and now covers an area of about 25,100 square metres.

Before Buddhism reached Tibet from India, the Bon religion was prevalent in Tibet. It originated in Shang Shung, a neighbouring country at the time Tibet emerged as a power in Central Asia. The Bon religion is a form of nature worship and the Bonpos, the followers of Bon, believe that spirits everywhere are both good and evil. The good spirits are worshipped and the evil ones propitiated with offerings of food, drink, clothing and stones. The Bon religion developed from a tribal cult into a highly evolved form with its own literature, doctrines, monasteries, teachings and rules of conduct and it flourished in Tibet till the 6th century AD, when the first wave of Buddhism entered Tibet.

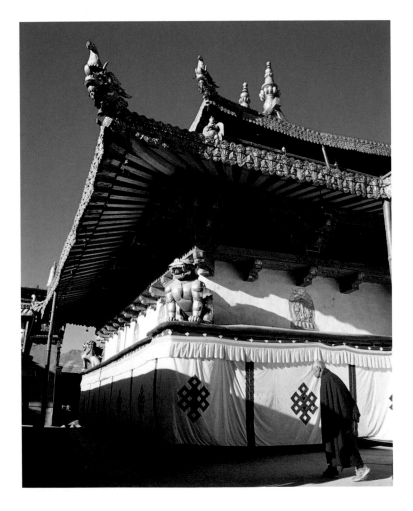

The intense rivalry between these schools of religion led to the collapse of the Tibetan state in AD 842. The Bonpo priesthood vanished only to emerge as an entirely different school in the 11th century AD. Though the Bonpo monks, like monks of other Tibetan Buddhist schools, strive to attain Buddhahood following the same path of scholastic study, ritual practice and meditational experience, there are superficial differences between Bonpos and Tibetan Buddhists. The Bonpos circumambulate holy places and holy objects keeping them to their left and turn their prayer wheels in a clockwise direction, their ritual chant being '*Om matri mu ye sale' du*', which has the same significance as the Buddhist '*Om mani padme hum*'.

By the 11th century AD, Buddhism had emerged as the leading religion in Tibet, with two principal schools, each differentiated by the colour of hats worn on ceremonial occasions. The 'Red Hats' belong to the non-reformed schools, from the Nyingmapas to the Kagyupas, while the 'Yellow Hats' denote the reformed school founded by Tsong Khapa, the Buddhist sage.

Built by Tsong Khapa in 1409 AD, the Ganden monastery in western Lhasa is the main monastery of the Gelugpa sect, 'Ganden' being the Tibetan name for the paradise of the Buddha of the Future. According to the scriptures, the arrival of this Buddha will herald the end of the world's sufferings, with the Ganden monastery as the route to the world's salvation.

Tsong Khapa, as the first abbot of Ganden monastery, was the appointed head of the Gelugpa sect. Even today, the abbot or *tripa* of Ganden monastery, rather than the Dalai Lama, leads this predominant sect and has traditionally been a strong candidate for the position of regent within the Tibetan government – for example, when the incumbent Dalai Lama was unable to rule.

About 2 kilometres north of Lhasa, at the base of Tatipu hill, is the Sera monastery. It was built in 1419 by Jamchen Chojey, one of Tsong Khapa's disciples. Spread over an area of twenty-eight acres, the monastery consists of the four-storeyed Coqen Hall, the main assembly hall, which is supported by 125 pillars of varying heights, and covers about 2000 square metres and five chapels honouring Buddhist icons Maitreya, Sakyamuni, Arhats, Tsong Khapa, and Kwan-yin. Gems to be found here include 105 out of the original 108 volumes of the Buddhist

Above: A view of the Jokhang temple, which has an area of 25,100 square metres and is the ultimate pilgrimage destination for Tibetan pilgrims.

Facing page: Ruins and reconstruction at Ganden monastery, once one of Tibet's largest religious centres with more than 100 temples and over 3500 monks.

classic *Gangyur* of Tripitaka in Tibetan. These priceless volumes are the earliest *sutra*s printed by engraving in China and contain the teachings of Buddha.

An unforgettable experience at Sera is to watch the monks debate each other in a large courtyard. As a part of their study of doctrines, Gelugpa or Yellow Hat Sect lamas participate in debates to further their comprehension and to proceed to more advanced levels of study. They begin as early as 3.00 a.m. and emphasize their debate points with heavy foot stomping and loud claps, in an animated debating style that is part of the time-honoured monastic educational system.

At the foot of the Mountain Gambo Utse, 5 kilometres west of Lhasa, is the Drepung monastery of the Gelugpa sect in Tibetan Buddhism. It covers an area of 250,000 square metres and in the past was home to nearly 10,000 monks. Seen from a distance, it resembles a heap of rice, which is the meaning of its name, Drepung. It was established in 1416 by Tsong Khapa's disciple, Jamchen Chojey, and has four sections, of which Loseling, or 'The Hermitage of the Radiant Mind', is the largest.

Two magnificent white pagodas form the centre of the cluster of buildings such as the *zhacang*s (Buddhist colleges) and *kamcun*s (dormitories for monks), while the Ganden Potrang, in the southwest corner of the monastery, was built under the supervision of the second Dalai Lama, Gedun Gyatso in 1530. It became the residence of successive Dalai Lamas. After the fifth Dalai Lama moved to the Potala Palace, it served as the meeting place for the local regime.

About 3 kilometres west of the Potala Palace is Norbulingka or the 'Jewelled Garden', which was built by Kelzang Gyatso, the seventh Dalai Lama, in 1755 and became the traditional summer residence for successive Dalai Lamas. The oldest building here is the Gesang Pozhang Palace. The gardens, with their fountains and pools, are popular as picnic spots and the Sho Dun or 'Yoghurt Festival' is held here in the beginning of August.

THE UNKNOWN TIBET
SKY BURIALS

Left: A monk reads from the *sutras* (holy texts) at a sky burial ceremony at Drigung.

Above: Bodies being offered during a sky burial ceremony at Drigung. Tibetans believe that one should benefit other beings at every stage of one's life. So, after death, corpses are offered to vultures that frequent the sky burial grounds.

A sky burial is one of the three principal ways in which the Tibetans traditionally return their dead to the earth, the other being cremation and water burial. A sky burial follows the ritual of 'jha-tor' or giving alms to birds. According to Tibetan belief, the spirit leaves the body at the moment of death, so a dead body is fed to vultures as a last token of charity. The beginnings of this ritual can perhaps be traced to the scarcity of soil and wood in Tibet.

There are about 1100 sky burial sites in Tibet, the largest site being at the Drigung Til monastery. The burial involves an ancient ritual carried out by a special class of people called the *rogyapas*. When a Tibetan dies, the corpse is kept for twenty-four hours in a sitting position while a lama recites prayers from the *Tibetan Book of the Dead*. These prayers are meant to speed the soul through the forty-nine levels of *bardo*, the state between death and rebirth. Three days after death, the body is blessed and carried on the back of a close friend to the durtro, or burial site. The *rogyapas*, dressed in long white aprons, then cut off the corpse's hair, chop up the body with knives, hatchets and heavy stones.

The organs are removed and set up for the encircling vultures, who are kept away with the help of sticks till the cutters give the signal. The men then step back and let the vultures approach the chopped body parts. Meanwhile, the bones are pounded to powder and then mixed with barley flour to invite the birds.

Tibetans believe that everyone should witness a sky burial at least once in life. This, they believe, teaches us the impermanence and ephemerality of life.

Above: Rock paintings at a sky burial site near Lhasa.

Facing page (top left, top right and bottom): Bodies being offered at a sky burial ceremony.

THE UNKNOWN TIBET
MT. KAILASH MANSAROVAR

Lying in the lap of Mount Kailash is the Mansarovar lake, considered the holiest spot in the Himalayas by followers of Hinduism, Buddhism and Jainism and the pre-Buddhist Bon religion. The name Mansarovar, in fact, means 'Lake of Consciousness and Enlightenment'. Buddhists regard Mount Kailash as the Kang Rinpoche, the 'Jewel of the Snows'. For them, Kailash is a gigantic natural *mandala*; it is the epicentre of all tantric forces. The Buddhists believe that Queen Maya, Buddha's mother, was carried here by the gods and washed before giving birth to Buddha. To the Bonpos, it is the 'Nine-storey Swastika Mountain', the mystic 'soul' of the entire region.

The sublime snow-clad Mount Kailash, soaring up to 6714 metres in the Nagri region of western Tibet, dwarfs all other peaks in the region, looking like a great cone of ice with a

A group of pilgrims circumambulate Mount Kailash. The 52-kilometre journey is completed by Tibetans generally in one day. While Hindus, Buddhists and Jains do the circumambulation in clockwise direction, those from the Bon faith walk in the anti-clockwise direction.

distinctive dome-shaped cap. Climbing the peak is prohibited for religious reasons. Pilgrims of several religions believe that circumambulating Mount Kailash on foot, known as a *kora*, or *parikrama*, brings good fortune. While Hindus and Buddhists walk in a clockwise direction to cover the 52-kilometre long circuit, the Bon people walk in a counter clockwise manner.

The trek, which is normally completed in three days, starts at Darchan. On the way, the route passes through Tarboche, where the annual flagpole-raising ceremony takes place during the Saga Dawa festival; Diraphuk, the site of a 13th-century monastery; and the Dolmala pass (5637 metres), the highest point in the trek. On the way down from the pass is Gauri Kund, a beautiful oval-shaped lake of the purest emerald hue. It has an interesting legend attached to it. It is said that when Goddess Parvati, wife of Lord Shiva, was bathing here, her son Ganesha stood guard. When Lord Shiva returned from Mount Kailash, Ganesha barred his way, which so angered him that he chopped off Ganesha's head. Later, repentant and berated by Parvati, Shiva requested a passing elephant to donate his head, which was then grafted on to Ganesha.

The next stop is at Zuthul Phuk gompa (*phuk* means cave), where Milarepa, Tibet's greatest teacher and saint, had once meditated, and the circuit ends at Mansarovar. To the west of Mansarovar is the Rakas Tal, where it is said that Ravana, the king of Lanka, had undertaken a period of penance to invoke Lord Shiva. Close to Mansarovar are a number of hot-water springs and a bath in the sulphur water goes a long way in removing all traces of tiredness after a long trek.

The Saga Dawa festival, held in Tarboche during the full moon (of the fourth lunar month) to mark the birth, transcendence and death of Buddha, is the most important festival in western Tibet. It is a carnival of Tibetan music, chanting and festivity, an event not to be missed. Tibetans from all over the country flock to the Mount Kailash for a prayer-flag ceremony when a giant flagpole is ritually taken down and the prayer flags changed for new ones. After the flagpole is upright again, the Tibetans try to tell the future by watching its position; if the pole stays straight it means happiness for all of Tibet. This ritual gives us a glimpse into the fascinating world of Tibetan beliefs and the intense faith that marks their life-affirming ceremonies.

A *dhami* (soothsayer) prays while standing knee-deep in the sacred Mansarovar lake, in the lap of Mount Kailash. The lake is the source of power for the *dhamis* as this is where their ancestors always came for rebirth and renewal.

SIKKIM
IN THE SHADOW OF THE KANCHENJUNGA

While the modern and the traditional co-exist easily in Gangtok, the capital of Sikkim, the original inhabitants of the state are the Lepchas, fascinating tribals who worship the Kanchenjunga, the world's third highest peak, as their guardian deity. Sikkim is also home to an amazing array of sacred lakes, including the Tsomgo and the Gurudongmar.

Preceding page 122: A Phodang monastery dancer, wearing a traditional costume, completes a step during the Kagyet dance festival. The dance symbolizes the destruction of evil forces and hopes for peace and prosperity in every Sikkimese home.

Preceding page 123: Young, novice Buddhist monks are curious about the outsiders clicking photographs within their monastery.

S wirls of mist veil the snow-capped Himalayan peaks here while lush green valleys and forests and a profusion of orchids add colour to the landscape. This is Sikkim, which in May 1975 became a part of India and Gangtok the capital of the twenty-second state of India. Since then, Gangtok has emerged as a magnet for tourists and travellers and a gateway into a state with a distinct cultural and religious identity. Here, in Gangtok, the traditional and the modern co-exist with remarkable ease.

Lying atop a ridge soaring to 1780 metres, Gangtok offers spectacular views of the world's third tallest peak – Kanchenjunga. Gangtok in the Bhutia language means 'a hillock cut out to make flat land'. It is the only urban town of note in the second smallest state of India in terms of area. The capital has its share of broad roads, flyovers, and neon-lit markets. What first catches the eye is the cleanliness of the town, where policemen – looking dashing in their felt hats and smart uniform – keep the crowds and traffic disciplined, unlike in other hill towns of the country. As in all hill stations, there is a Mall Road, officially named the Mahatma

Left: Prayer flags flutter at Tashiding monastery in west Sikkim, while the sun shines on Mount Kanchenjunga rising above the clouds in the background.

Top: A decorated pillar in front of a Buddha statue in Gangtok, the capital of Sikkim.

Gandhi Marg, which is the centre of activity. The shops and hotels lining the Mall Road are painted in bright reds and yellows, mimicking the colours of the mythical dragon. And, as even a casual observer will note, every third shop is a liquor shop displaying a plethora of brands – which is understandable as Sikkim is one of the largest producers of liquor in the country.

The heart of Gangtok has three bazaars – the Old, the New and the Lal Bazaar. The Old and New Bazaars are situated on the Mahatma Gandhi Road. This is where the shopping centres, restaurants, hotels, banks and cyber cafes are located. The Lal Bazaar was set up in the 1950s to enable the villagers to sell their products at the local fair, usually held on Sundays and the bazaar

is named after J.S. Lal, the first dewan (minister) of Sikkim. It is at the Lal Bazaar that the traditional and the modern merge seamlessly. Various ethnic groups from different villages gather here to buy, sell or just gossip, bringing with them all the colours of Sikkim under one roof.

Gangtok has a lot more on offer for the curious visitor. The 200-year-old Enchey monastery, located on a hilltop above Gangtok, is well worth the 3-kilometre climb. This monastery belongs to the Nyingmapa order and was once the hermitage site of Lama Drupthob Karpo, said to have had the power of flying. The Do-Drul chorten, a stupa built by Trulsi Rimpoche in 1945–46, is encircled by 108 prayer wheels and is one of the most

important and biggest stupas found in Sikkim. The stupa houses many revered religious objects, including holy books and two huge statues of Guru Rimpoche, or Guru Padmasambhava. Every year, in January, a religious masked dance is performed here with great fanfare for two days.

The Ridge, a small stretch of plain and flat road above the town of Gangtok, is about a fifteen-minute walk from the main market. The White Hall and the chief minister's official residence, known as the Mintokgang (Blossomed Crowned Hilltop), stand at one end and the beautifully designed Palace Gate with a pagoda roof-top on the other. The two-storeyed White Hall, built in 1932 in a typical British architectural style, is so-called not because it is painted white, but because it was constructed in memory of the first political officer of Sikkim, Claude White. Near it is the Flower Show Hall, where there are exhibitions of fabulous seasonal flowers throughout the year.

Wherever you are in Sikkim, you cannot escape the presence of the world's third-highest peak, Kanchenjunga (8586 metres), or Khangchendzonga as it is locally called. In Gangtok, Tashi View Point, 6 kilometres from the town, is the best place to view the breathtaking panorama of the majestic Kanchenjunga peak and the surrounding hills. Built by the late king of Sikkim, Tashi Namgyal, the Point is situated on the North Sikkim Highway and has a resting shed and a small cafeteria.

Another spot for a spectacular view of the Kanchenjunga is Hanuman Tok, a temple devoted to Lord Hanuman, the monkey god, about 5 kilometres above White Hall on a bifurcation off the Gangtok-Nathula Highway. The route also offers stunning views of Gangtok and the adjoining hills. A short distance from the steps leading to the Hanuman temple is the cremation ground of the erstwhile royal family of Sikkim, with its many stunning stupas and chortens.

Also on a hillock above the Gangtok-Nathula road is Ganesh Tok, a temple dedicated to Lord Ganesh, the Hindu elephant-headed deity. The temple is so small that it can barely accommodate one person and visitors have to crawl to get inside it. The 205-hectare Himalayan Zoological Park (also known as Bulbuley) just opposite Ganesh Tok extends almost up to the Hanuman Tok. A paved cement path passes by fenced open-air enclosures housing red pandas, barking deer, bear and other animals of Sikkim in a semi-natural habitat.

A visit to Rumtek monastery, 24 kilometres away on a bifurcation from the Gangtok-Siliguri Highway, is an unforgettable experience. Built in 1960 by the sixteenth Gyalwa Karmapa, it presents an imposing sight. A replica of the original Kagyurpa monastery in Tsurphu, Tibet, it now functions as the headquarters of the Dharma Chakra Religious Centre. Inside the complex, the full force of Tibetan Buddhism strikes you. The followers go about their spiritual business with vibrant energy and the monastery compound is visually a beehive of activity. Spinning prayer wheels, bowed heads, musicians, children and old wizened faithfuls, all come together in a whirl of colours and religious fervour.

About 125 kilometres from here, in the western part of the state, is Yuksom, the birthplace of Sikkim as a kingdom nearly 400 years ago. On the way, perched atop a hill rising above the confluence of the Rangit and Rathong rivers, is the Tashiding monastery. It takes a 2-kilometre walk to reach the monastery on a track that winds through an ancient forest aflame with orchids. The bright reds and golden yellows of the monastery vie with the green of the forest around it. A profusion of prayer flags encircles the monastery and adjacent to the main monastery is an enclosure of a group of chortens, including a golden one. They are enclosed with an amazing wall, every inch of which is covered with carvings of Buddha in different poses and sacred stones in myriad colours.

Tashiding, which belongs to the Nyingmapa sect, comes alive at midnight of the fourteenth and fifteenth of the first

Tibetan month (falling usually in January–February). It is the time when the sacred ceremony of Bumchu is performed here – *bum* means 'pot or vase' while *chu* means 'water'. During this festival the lamas of the monastery open a pot containing the holy water. If the water is full to the brim, it prophesies bloodshed and disturbances and if it is empty or almost dry, it signifies famine. If it is half full, it foretells a year in which peace and prosperity will prevail. The pot is later replenished with river water and sealed at the end of the festival, to be opened only in the next Bumchu.

From Tashiding, Yuksom is just 20 kilometres away. Gigantic waterfalls cascade near the road, which passes through some breathtaking scenery on this stretch. Yuksom is an overgrown village with a small market and lush green barley fields. The hills and valleys abound with numerous orchids, primulas, rhododendrons and marigolds as well as magnolia and cherry trees.

The road ends here, but ahead are the trekking trails to the lakes and peaks above. At the end of the road is the place from where the recent history of Sikkim begins – the coronation throne of Norbugang. The stone throne was where Phuntshog was coronated as the first chogyal of Sikkim by the great Nyingmapa lama Lhatsun Chembo and two other lamas. It was here that Sikkim became a kingdom, right under an ancient giant juniper tree, the stem lined with orchids, and in front of a huge chorten, believed to contain soil and water from all over Sikkim. In a way, Yuksom, which means 'where the three lamas met', embodies the spirit of Sikkim – simple, open and bountiful.

Preceding pages 126–127: Kanchenjunga from Kaluk Bazaar in Sikkim. Kanchenjunga, which means 'The Five Treasures of Snows', is the third-highest mountain in the world with an altitude of 8586 metres.

Facing page: Rumtek monastery, near Gangtok, is the largest in Sikkim. It is one of the most important seats of the Kagyu lineage outside Tibet.

Top left: The colourful entrance to a small monastery in a village near Gangtok.

Top right: Prag Chu river winds through the snow wastes near Goechala, at an altitude of 5456 metres. Kanchenjunga is visible in the background.

THE UNKNOWN SIKKIM
LEPCHAS

The original inhabitants of Sikkim are said to be Lepchas, who have now become a minority, with Bhutias and people of Nepalese origin outnumbering them. The Lepchas have Mongoloid features and refer to themselves as Rongpas, or 'ravine-dwellers' in their own language. They say that 'Lepcha' is a mispronunciation of Lap-che, a name given to them by Nepali speakers. Though they can be found all over Sikkim, they are mainly concentrated in the Dzongu valley in the northern part of Sikkim. Before adopting Buddhism or Christianity as their religion, the earliest Lepcha settlers were believers in the 'Bon' faith, based on spirits, good and bad, that emanated from the natural world – spirits of mountains, rivers and forests.

The traditional Lepcha dress for men is called a 'pagi', half-pajamas under a robe made of striped cotton that resembles a loose jacket. The robe comes to the knees and is pinned on the shoulder and tied around the waist. An integral part of the dress is a 'ban' or 'payak', the traditional Lepcha knife. A Lepcha woman wears a two-piece dress, comprising a full-sleeved blouse called a 'tago' and a skirt called 'domdyan', with a scarf tied around the head.

The Lepchas' highly developed language is known as Rong, the origin of its script being shrouded in myth. Some Lepchas believe that it was invented by Thekong Mensalong, a legendary Lepcha

Facing page and following pages 132–133: Buddhist monks from Lepcha community in their full headgear, and with musical instruments, pray to the Lord.

Left and following page 133: A Lepcha *bomthing*, or priest, uses millet beer to capture spirits.

figure who lived in the beginning of the 17th century, but the more accepted view is that it was invented by the third king of the Namgyal dynasty, Chador Namgyal, in the 18th century. The language falls under the Tibeto-Burman group of languages and does not have its roots in Sanskrit, like the other tribal dialects of India, Bhutan and Nepal. It is also unique because it is one of the few tribal languages with a script of its own.

The Lepcha house, or '*li*', is rectangular in shape and usually made of bamboo. Lepchas are excellent weavers and also adept in bamboo and cane weaving. Their major festival is Namsoong (also called Lossong), which marks the beginning of the Lepcha new year and is celebrated for a week. Traditionally, a couple of minutes before the beginning of the new year, a Lepcha priest, referred to as '*bomthing*' performs rituals by offering '*chi fut*', or alcoholic beverages, to the spirits and at midnight, the effigy of the demon king, Laso Mung Punu is burnt. During the Namsoong period, the Lepchas burn incense with butter and seeds of the *Oroxylum indicum*, or Indian trumpet flower, early in the morning.

Lepchas worship the Kanchenjunga as their guardian deity, pointing to their 'Bon' traditions. Pang Lhabsol is the festival to celebrate the powers of the mountain and is held on the fifteenth day of the seventh month of the Tibetan calendar, corresponding to late August and early September. A week before the customary masked and warrior dances are performed, the lamas of Pemayangtse monastery, near Yuksom, offer prayers, invoking Mount Kanchenjunga to protect the land and look after the people.

THE UNKNOWN SIKKIM
THE LAKES

Sikkim has an amazing array of lakes within its borders, most of which are held sacred by the people. The easiest one to visit is Tsomgo lake, also called Changu lake, which is on the Gangtok-Nathula road in east Sikkim, the last point where foreign travellers are allowed to go just before the Indo-Chinese border at Nathula, where the two armies patrol at a handshaking distance. Permission has to be taken in advance and only Indian tourists are allowed to visit the pass on specific days of the week. The magnificent Tsomgo lake is 38 kilometres from Gangtok, and is open to all tourists. It is at an altitude of 3780 metres and about one kilometre in length. It bursts suddenly on the scene as the road takes a turn, the only clue for the visitor being a trickle of water from a crack. Considered the 'head' of all lakes in Sikkim, it is very sacred for the local people. The lake remains frozen throughout the winter and up to the end of April, and if you are lucky you may catch some snowfall in May. The birdlife here is vibrant, with thrushes, redstarts and forktails in abundance. In winter, the lake also hosts the brahminy ducks, which come all the way from the central plains of Asia to roost here.

Right and following pages 136–137: Tsomgo lake, literally meaning 'Source of the Lake' in the Bhutia language, lies 38 kilometres from Gangtok at an altitude of 3780 metres. This oval lake freezes in winter while in summer it supports a wide variety of plant and bird life.

In west Sikkim, at an altitude of 1800 metres, is the Khecheopalri lake. It is nearly 120 kilometres from Sikkim and the nearest town is Pelling (34 kilometres). Khecheopalri (which means the Wishing Lake) is sacred to the Lepchas and the Hindus alike. The Khecheopalri village and the gompa are just 3 kilometres from the lake. The water in this lake is placid and crystal clear. From the top of the ridge, the reward for the climb is an excellent view of Mount Pandim (6691metres). A trekkers' hut has been built near the lake for tourists.

The Gurudongmar lake in north Sikkim is the largest and one of the highest lakes in Sikkim. It is 190 kilometres from Gangtok and at an altitude of 5200 metres. Amazingly, it is accessible by road. The lake lies on the northern side of the Khangchengyao range high in the Tibetan plateau and the stream emerging from it is one of the sources of the Teesta river. The lake is named after Guru Padmasambhava, who is said to have brought Tantric Buddhism to Tibet in the 9th century. According to a legend, since the lake remained frozen most of the year, it was not possible to drink its water. When Guru Padmasambhava passed by while returning from Tibet, the local residents are reported to have asked him to give them a source of water. The Guru obliged and even today, a portion of the lake does not freeze in the extreme winter. Although the milky-white water of the lake is considered sacred, the extremely inhospitable surrounding terrain makes it difficult to reach the place and the lake sees only a handful of visitors each year. But for those who do reach the stark, snowswept plateau, it is an experience never to forget.

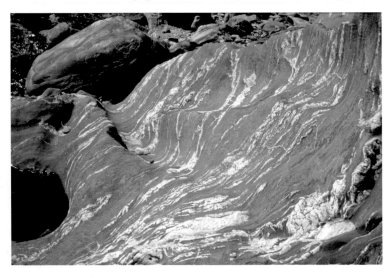

Above: The Teesta river is one of the fastest flowing rivers in Asia and is the main river of Sikkim.

BHUTAN
VEILED IN THE MISTS OF TIME

Remaining aloof from the rest of the world for centuries, Bhutan is the only truly 'mystical' country in Asia. The valleys and mountains of this pristine land house spectacular monasteries and dzongs, such as the Taktshang monastery. Perched precariously on a 900-metre high cliff, the monastery is one of the most sacred Buddhist sites in the world.

Preceding page 138: Taktshang monastery is situated at one of the most spectacular sites in the Himalayas and is the most venerated in Bhutan. It is a set of temples built in the 17th century on a vertical cliff.

Preceding page 139: Monks unroll a huge *thangka* or *thongdrel* representing the Shabdrung, Bhutan's great ruler, at the Punakha festival.

Preceding pages 140–141: Next to the traditionally painted wooden windows of a house, is a bright red painting of a phallus, a common sight in Bhutan. The painted phallus, it is believed, protects those who live inside the house and wards off the evil eye.

The only truly 'mystical' country in Asia, Bhutan has managed to keep a lid on itself and has revealed its treasures in a miserly way to the outside world in order to protect the country's environment and cultural traditions. However, this has only made it more alluring.

The Bhutanese call their country Druk Yul, or 'The Land of the Thunder Dragon'. Its capital, Thimpu, remains the only capital city of the world without traffic lights – they were replaced by traffic policemen as people found them too 'impersonal'. This small gesture demonstrates the say people have in this nation, which has begun its change from a monarchy to a parliamentary democracy with its first elections in 2008, and shows that the country invests more in 'Gross National Happiness', a term employed by the King of Bhutan in 1972 when quizzed about Gross National Produce (GNP) of the country.

Thimpu is the most populated place of Bhutan, with nearly one lakh people. At an altitude of 2350 metres, Thimpu sits in a valley on the banks of the Wang Chu river. With the gradual opening up of the country in the new millennium, construction activity is booming in Thimpu and numerous shops, restaurants,

Left: Dancers performing the Dramitse Nga Chham dance, also called the Drum from Dramitse, during the Buddhist festival of Paro Tsechu held at the dzong in Paro.

Top: The impressive Trongsa dzong, which is the ancestral home of the royal family. Built in 1644 on a mountain spur high above the gorges of the Mangde Chhu, the dzong controlled east-west trade for centuries.

retail stores, apartment buildings and houses are coming up everywhere. Here too, is a visible difference from the rest of the world's expanding cities, for all buildings follow the traditional style with colourful Buddhist paintings and motifs on the walls.

Among the many places to be seen and admired in Thimpu is the imposing pink-roofed Tashichhodzong, 'The Fortress of the Glorious Religion', in which the National Assembly meets. It hosts a masked-dance festival called Tse Chu, at the end of summer. It was built in 1641 and reconstructed in 1962. The royal premises are at a short distance from Thimpu, at Dechencholing, a three-storeyed palace built in the traditional style with beautifully landscaped lawns studded with ponds, fountains and willow trees. Other landmarks of Thimpu are the monastery of Tangu Cherry, the Memorial Chorten dedicated to the third King of Bhutan, Jigme Dorji Wangchuck, and the National Library built in the style of a traditional temple.

Paro, the other big town of Bhutan, lies in the valley named after it. It also has the country's only airport. Paro valley is known for its natural beauty with its verdant fields and abundant orchards nourished by the glacial water of the Paro Chu river and it is here that the gleaming white Phobjika glacier lies. Overlooking the Paro town is Rinpung dzong, an elegant fortress set on a knoll across the Paro Chu river that offers spellbinding views of the valley. Its location is symbolic as it is the focal point of all religious and social activities in the valley. Close to the fortress is yet another castle, the Ta dzong. Bhutan's national museum is housed here and it has invaluable artefacts depicting the country's national heritage. In the northern part of the valley is Druguel dzong, or the 'Victorious Fortress'. It was here that the Tibetan army was repelled by the Bhutanese in the 17th century.

Dzongs or fortresses are peculiar to this Himalayan kingdom, their architectural grandeur expressed in height and

Top: Bird's-eye view of Jakar dzong showing how the courtyards and buildings are constructed along the ridge. Jakar is the administrative district of the Bhumthang area in central Bhutan.

Facing page (left): An aerial view of the Dechencholing Royal Palace in Thimpu, home of the King or 'Druk Gyalpo' (Dragon King) of Bhutan.

Facing page (right): Paro dzong, one of Bhutan's strongest and most strategic fortresses, is built on a rocky outcrop, at an altitude of just over 2100 metres.

massiveness even as they remain gracefully elegant in structure. Lama Gyalwa Lhanangpa from Tibet is credited with introducing dzongs into Bhutan in the 12th century. According to experts, the earlier dzongs served mainly a religious purpose but later, Zhabdrung Ngawang Namgyal gave another dimension to the dzong system. He built almost all the principal dzongs in Bhutan – Simtokha, Tongsa, Punakha, Wangdiphodrang, Gasa, Tashichhodzong, and the Rinpung dzong at Paro – as strongholds to check Tibetan inroads into Bhutan. They soon became a focal point of all Bhutanese activities, whether social, military, administrative or monastic.

Mostly located on a mountain spur, a dzong usually overlooks a valley, while its watchtowers and observation posts are strategically placed on the highest point. If the dzong is built on the side of a valley slope, a smaller dzong or watchtower is typically built directly uphill from the main dzong so that the slope is kept clear of attackers who might otherwise shoot downward into the courtyard of the main dzong below.

In architectural style, dzongs resemble Lhasa's great Potala Palace, with their high, inward-sloping walls painted white. Usually there is a red ochre stripe near the top of the walls and the temples within have Chinese-style flared roofs made of hardwood and bamboo. The stone-laid courtyards are approached by massive staircases and narrow defensible entrances with large wooden doors.

Facing page: A Black Hat dancer at the Punakha festival that takes place in early spring every year.

Above: A house on a hill overlooks a meandering river at Wangdiphodrang that is situated at the junction of the Mo Chu and the Tang Chu rivers. This valley is also called 'Windy' Phodrang by the locals because of the strong gusts of wind that are characteristic of this region.

THE UNKNOWN BHUTAN
TAKTSHANG
MONASTERY

The crowning glory of the Paro valley is the Taktshang monastery, perched almost precariously on a 900-metre high cliff, which rises as a steep wall from the valley below. At an altitude of nearly 3120 metres, the monastery truly lives up to its name, which means 'Tiger's Nest', for this is where Padmasambhava (also known as Guru Rimponche, the Buddhist sage who is said to have brought Tantric Buddhism to Tibet in the 9th century) is believed to have flown on the back of a tiger to meditate on this spot. Other famous visitors to the monastery included Ngawang Namgyal in the 17th century and Milarepa, the highly revered Tibetan saint. Taktshang is thus a holy place visited by pilgrims from all over Bhutan and is one of the most revered Buddhist sacred sites in the world.

Top: A view of the Taktshang monastery near Paro. It is said that the original cave here was blessed by Padmasambhava, the famed master who brought Buddhism to Tibet in the 9th century.

Facing page (bottom): Costumed dancers participate in the celebration of the eight manifestations of Guru Padmasambhava, during a festival at Zhemgang dzong.

On 19 April 1998, a fire destroyed the monastery's main structure but the Dubkhang, its most sacred sanctum, was found to be intact and a number of its most precious relics and treasures were retrieved. The monastery today has been restored to its original splendour, though tourists cannot enter it and are stopped from going further than 100 metres from the pilgrimage centre.

The monastery can be reached only on foot or on a mule. The trek begins 8 kilometres north of Paro, passing through a thick blue-pine forest at first. Then comes a stream and it is after crossing it that the steep climb of 370 metres up the ridge starts, continuing to a small chorten with prayer flags in a riot of colours. A short level walk then brings the visitor to a cafeteria. From the cafeteria it is another forty-five-minute uphill walk to Taktshang. The monastery seems to grow out of the rock-face and is definitely a highlight for any trip to Bhutan.

Above: A dancer wears a mask of a dragon, the symbol of Bhutan, at a religious festival.

Right: A man blows a trumpet on a cliff facing the Taktshang monastery, also known as the Tiger's Nest.

ARUNACHAL

WHERE THE SUN RISES FIRST

Temples, forts, forests, shrines and monasteries dot the Himalayan hills of Arunachal Pradesh. And deep in the rainforests of the Patkai hills live the Noctes and Wanchos, the last of the head hunters in the world.

Preceding page 152: The giant gilded statue of Lord Buddha at the Tawang monastery. Over 8 metres tall, the statue is among the tallest Buddhas in India.

Preceding page 153: A portrait of an Apatani woman with nose plugs, or *yaping hullo* as they are called. The women of the Apatani pastoral tribe used to wear nose plugs to look unattractive to neighbouring tribes. Today, the practice is losing its following.

As dawn begins to cast its first glow, this is where the sun rises first in India – in Arunachal Pradesh, the most eastern of the Himalayan states. As Arunachal is at the end of the Himalayan range, the state's landscape has a different feel, with its tropical rainforests mixed with Himalayan vistas. It is the largest state in the North-East region of India, which includes six other states – Assam, Meghalaya, Manipur, Nagaland, Tripura and Sikkim.

Nestling between two Himalayan hills, at a mean altitude of 350 metres, is Itanagar, the capital of the state. The history of Itanagar can be traced back to the 11th century, some historical accounts identifying it with Mayapur, the capital of the Jiti dynasty that ruled the region at the time. Arunachal Pradesh also finds mention in the *Kalika Purana* and in the epics of *Mahabharata* and *Ramayana*. It is believed that the sage Vyas meditated here. The town got its present name from the Ita fort (*ita* means brick) here that dates back to the 14th or 15th century.

Apart from the fort, there are many places worth visiting in and around Itanagar. On one of the hilltops is a Buddhist temple, with a beautiful yellow roof that shows a Tibetan influence. The

Left: A typical scene in the misty hills of Namdapha National Park, which was declared as a tiger reserve by the government in 1983.

Top: A ritual masked dance by members of the Sherdukpen tribe in Arunachal's Kameng district.

shrine offers spellbinding views of the town and its surroundings. Then, 6 kilometres away from the capital, is the famous Gyakar Sinyi, or the Ganga lake, a popular picnic spot. Set amidst a verdant forest, the ethereal-looking lake mirrors the tall trees sheltering orchid blooms and lush vegetation that abounds in colourful flowers and an amazing variety of herbs.

Bomdila, the district headquarters of West Kameng district, is just a few hours climb away in the northwestern part of the state. At 3500 metres in the Himalayas, Bomdila offers panoramic views of Himalayan peaks, apart from an enchanting landscape dotted with apple orchards and Buddhist monasteries. It is spread over a wide ridge that straddles a mountain and offers a bird's-eye

view of the Kangto and Gorichen peaks, the highest in the state. Also at Bomdila are the Gaden Rabgeling and Thubchog Gatseling monasteries.

Bomdila is said to be the coldest town in this region, the icy weather a gift from the surrounding snow-clad mountains. A cold breeze during the day, chilling to the bone, is a rule here rather than an exception. The mountains and valleys here make Bomdila a hub of hiking activity in the Kameng region. A number of treks and hikes into the mountains, ranging from easy day-long trails to treks needing weeks, start from the town.

The main gompa here is the Bomdila or the Gentse Gaden Rabgyel Ling monastery. It was built by the twelfth reincarnation

Facing page (top): A tribal mask. Each tribe in Arunachal Pradesh has its unique set of masks.

Above right: A bird's-eye view of the 17th-century Tawang monastery, one of the largest of the Mahayana sect in Asia.

Above: A shaman belonging to the Tagin tribe poses with his sword.

of Tsona Gontse Rinpoche in 1965 and is a replica of the Tsona Gontse monastery at Tsona in south Tibet, which was established during the 15th century.

The road via Tse-La takes you to Tawang. The route itself is an attraction as it is the world's second-highest motorable road – after Khardungla in Ladakh. On the other side is Tawang, known for its monastery, one of the largest of the Mahayana sect in Asia. It is enclosed by a compound wall and has an ancient library that boasts of many rare books and manuscripts. Built some time in the 17th century, Tawang monastery is the fountainhead of the spiritual life of the followers of the Gelugpa sect of the Mahayana school of Buddhism and about 300 lamas reside and study here.

The highlight of the monastery is a giant gilded statue of Lord Buddha. Over 8 metres high, the statue is among the tallest Buddhas in India.

Close to Itanagar is the Namdapha National Park. Covering an area of 1985 square kilometres, it lies at the extreme end of Arunachal Pradesh, bordering Myanmar on two sides and watered by the Noa-Dehing and Namdapha rivers. A legally protected area, it is the largest National Park in the North-East of India and is a tiger reserve.

More than half of Namdapha is still virgin territory as virtually no one has set foot in most tracts of this 1985-square kilometre natural park. And for those who are not too adventurous, just basking in the idea of exploring even a corner of the country's most diverse forest landscape is reward enough, with its altitudinal variation from 200 to 4500 metres and rich flora, ranging from the peninsular to the alpine. Adding to the enchantment is its rich wildlife. A few species like the hoolock gibbon, Namdapha flying squirrel, white wing wood duck and Namdapha shortwing bird are endemic to the region. Namdapha is also home to the rare red panda.

It is the celebrated cat family that draws most visitors to the Park. Namdapha is probably the country's only national park where nine different cat species can be found. Apart from the king cat, there are three more avatars of the big cat: the very elusive snow leopard, the clouded leopard and the common leopard, together with a remarkable number of lesser cats, such as the Mexican spotted cat, black leopard, and the leopard, jungle, marbled, golden and fishing cats.

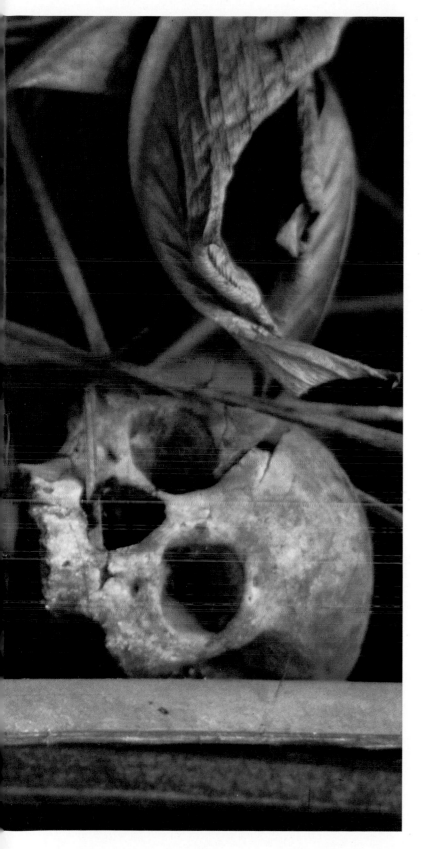

THE UNKNOWN ARUNACHAL
HEAD HUNTERS

Boar tusks and bear fur adorn the cane hats of the Noctes and Wanchos of Arunachal Pradesh, tribal warriors who live mainly in the forest and survive on its bounty. Hunting in the thick rainforests of the Patkai hills and along the border between India and Burma, tribal hunters look out for boar, deer and wild buffaloes, while taking on bears, leopards, tigers and other big game as well.

Leopard and tiger teeth hang as talismans from the costumes of hunters who have survived encounters with these predators, while beads made from bone and stone indicate status and wealth. The more flamboyant among them sport the plumage of hornbills and even eagles.

Not one among the warriors is squeamish about wearing human talismans. Internecine wars between the villages and different tribes have often resulted in the warring parties taking the heads of the vanquished and the skulls are usually displayed in the hut of the tribe's chieftain. Trophies in the form of gibbon or monkey skulls are also carried with aplomb by warriors, who are proud of their prowess.

With the passage of time, the Wancho area has become the main centre of woodcarving in Arunachal Pradesh. Wancho woodcarving was earlier associated with head hunting and human heads dominated everything that they made. But now, the subjects have diversified. Similarly, Nocte girls have come to be known for bead work.

The Noctes and Wanchos live in forested hills, with clouds clinging to the trees, and among giant ferns, wild banana groves and thickets of bamboo, living in harmony with nature as their tribes have always done – for centuries.

Human skulls of enemies killed in battle are placed as trophies on a skull rack inside the *morung*, a bachelor's dormitory of the Nocte tribe. Till the mid-20th century, head-taking was central to the Noctes, and a bachelor needed to capture a head before being considered eligible for marriage.

Corbis

Back cover, 4 (bottom left and right), 5 (middle right), 5 (bottom right), 8, 16-17, 18-19, 20, 21 (all), 23 (middle), 25 (bottom left), 26-27, 28, 29 (bottom), 33 (all), 37 (all), 57, 61, 64 (bottom), 65 (all), 66, 66-67, 68 (all), 69 (all), 70, 73 (all), 75, 78, 80-81, 85, 89, 94, 97 (bottom), 102, 102-103, 104, 105, 107, 109, 111, 113, 114, 116, 117 (bottom), 118-119, 128, 131, 132, 139, 140-141, 142-143, 143, 144-145 (all), 146, 146-147, 148 (bottom), 150, 150-151, 153, 156, 158-159, 160

Dinodia

41, 45, 46, 47 (bottom), 48-49 (bottom), 49 (top right), 54, 55, 56, 59 (top), 60-61, 62-63, 64 (top left and right), 72, 74, 76-77, 79 (all), 82-83, 87, 88, 122, 129 (all), 136, 136-137, 156-157

Getty

1, 5 (top right), 9, 10, 11 (bottom), 12-13, 14, 15, 22, 24-25 (top), 25 (bottom right), 32, 38 (bottom), 58, 59 (bottom), 90, 92, 93, 94-95, 96 (all), 106, 123, 124-125, 125, 126-127, 130, 132-133, 138, 148-149 (top)

India Pictures

4 (top right), 11 (top), 29 (top), 38 (top left and right), 40, 44-45, 49 (top left), 82, 86, 134-135, 152, 154-155, 155, 157 (top)

Javed Dar

42-43, 47 (top and middle)

Roli Collection

70-71, 84, 159 (bottom)

Shailendra Pandey

50, 50-51, 52 (both), 53

Thomas Kelly

Cover, 2-3, 4 (top left), 5 (top left), 5 (middle left), 5 (bottom left), 6-7, 23 (top and bottom), 30-31, 31 (all), 34-35, 36, 39, 77, 91, 97 (top), 98-99, 100, 101, 108-109, 110, 112, 114-115, 117 (top left and right), 120-121

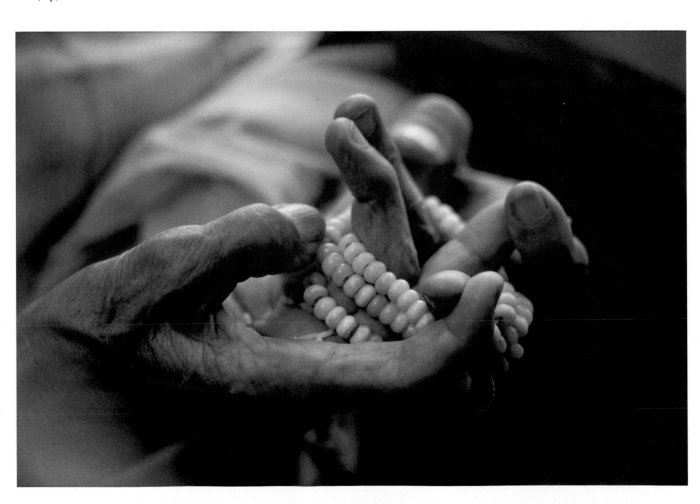

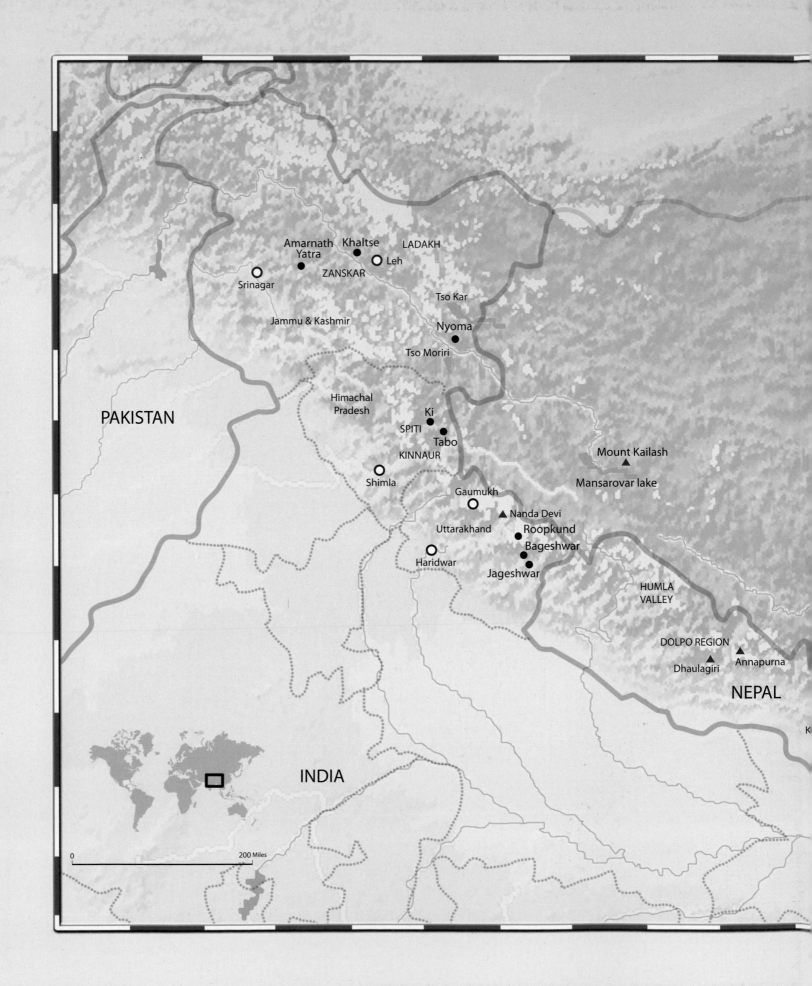